Moneo / Wettstein

Grand Hyatt – B e r l i n

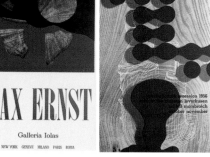

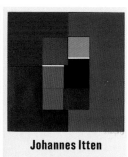

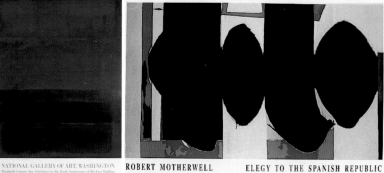

Plakate, die in Fluren, Mini- und Singlebed-Suiten hängen. Die Auswahl spannt einen
Bogen von der Avant-Garde der zwanziger Jahre zur Gegenwartskunst.

Moneo / Wettstein

Grand Hyatt – Berlin

Birkhäuser – Publishers for Architecture
Basel • Boston • Berlin

Konzept und Koordination / **Concept and Coordination:**
Klaus Leuschel, Zürich

Mit Fotos von / **With Photos by:**
Hélène Binet, London

Design-Konzept und Layout / **Design Concept and Layout:**
Gion-Men Kruegel-Hanna, Jane McDonald, Ithaca (New York, USA)

Übersetzung ins Englische / **Translation into English:**
Robin Benson, Berlin

A CIP catalogue record for this book is available from the Library of Congress,
Washington D.C., USA.

Deutsche Bibliothek Cataloging-in-Publication Data
Rafael Moneo, Hannes Wettstein - Grand Hyatt Berlin / [Übers. ins Engl.: Robin Benson]. -
Basel; Boston; Berlin: Birkhäuser, 2000
ISBN 3-7643-6104-2

© 2000 Birkhäuser – Publishers for Architecture, P.O. Box 133, CH-4010 Basel, Switzerland.
Printed on acid-free paper produced of chlorine-free pulp. TCF ∞
Printed in Germany
ISBN 3-7643-6104-2

9 8 7 6 5 4 3 2 1

Grand Hyatt – B e r l i n

Im Angedenken an all jene Wegbereiter, die der Hotellerie in der Vergangenheit neue Wege eröffnet haben: namentlich Cäsar Ritz und Auguste Escoffier als herausragende Vorbilder der Gastlichkeit

In memory of all those pioneers who set new trends in the hotel business: namely, Cäsar Ritz and Auguste Escoffier, who provided outstanding examples of hospitality

The Grand Hyatt Berlin is the American Hyatt Corporation's first five-star hotel on the Old Continent. But what do we mean by 'luxury hotel' nowadays? Willing hands always at one's beck and call, wherever one happens to be? An aristocratic setting with valuable furniture, as well as draperies and floral decoration? Or is not the expression 'luxury hotel' simply an anachronism these days, in any case?

After all, the image that comes to mind of the luxury hotel was formed during the transition from the 19th to the 20th century. For the very first time, thanks to the railways, a well-heeled clientele was in a position to retire to a natural paradise for a while, depending on the prevailing seasonal climate and individual preferences. Consequently, in their external appearance, the first luxury hotels situated in the Alps and at fashionable seaside resorts had more in common with the palaces and the residences of their select guests, who arrived in droves, than with functional buildings that have been purpose-built ever since to provide temporary hospitality.

It is important remember this fact in order to understand, in the light of social changes, the questions facing architects and interior designers in Berlin at the end of the 20th century and following the fall of the Wall. Furthermore, that very clientele whose status and wealth has tradi-

tionally provided the raison d'être behind luxury hotels has generally shown a preference for establishments with a history at least as long as that of their own family residences.

Against this background, one cannot heap enough praise on the approach adopted by the operators, since they have not even attempted to evoke or reproduce a world of imagery that awakens nostalgic memories of the past. The operators have certainly benefited from the Potsdamer Platz location. Further-more, the masterplan for the site, generally seen as a prime investment choice in the heart of this once-divided city, was designed by the Genoese architect, Renzo Piano. And Rafael Moneo, from Madrid, has shown considerable reserve in his design for the Grand Hyatt, which he has slotted masterfully into Renzo Piano's plan.

When one first sees the Grand Hyatt Berlin from the outside, it seems quite demure, and one can safely assume that it was meant to have this effect. Since Adolf Loos, at the very latest, luxury can hardly assume the form of an opulent exterior. In this respect, Rafael Moneo and his partner, Hannes Wettstein (now residing in Zurich) were only being consistent in concentrating on producing an interior design that would provide guests with an island retreat, revealing its qualities to them when they occupy their rooms and suites.

Hence, the lobby is like a refuge, shielding visitors from the hustle and the bustle of the outside world whilst, at the same time (as a journalist on the spot spontaneously put it), suggesting something of that cosmopolitanism of other >p.8

Das Grand Hyatt Berlin ist das erste Fünfstern-Hotel des amerikanischen Hyatt-Konzerns auf dem Alten Kontinent. Was aber meint heute «Luxushotel»? Dienstbare Hände immer und überall? Eine aristokratische Kulisse mit wertvollem Mobiliar, Draperien und Blumenschmuck? Oder handelt es sich heute nicht schon bei dem Wort «Luxushotel» um einen Anachronismus?

Geprägt wurde das Bild der Luxushotels schließlich durch die Zeit des Übergangs vom 19. ins 20. Jahrhundert. Erstmals war es damals einer vermögenden Klientel dank der Eisenbahn möglich, sich zeitweise und in Entsprechung zu den klimatischen Bedingungen der jeweiligen Jahreszeiten oder individuellen Vorlieben in landschaftliche Paradiese zurückzuziehen. Folglich auch glichen die ersten Luxushotels in den Alpen und an mondänen Badeorten nicht nur äußerlich mehr den Palästen und Residenzen ihrer erlesenen Gästeschar, als sie – bis heute – etwas mit funktionalen Zweckbauten temporärer Gastlichkeit gemein haben.

Dies gilt es in Erinnerung zu rufen, um in Anbetracht des gesellschaftlichen Wandels verstehen zu können, welcher Fragestellung Architekt und Raumgestalter sich in Berlin am Ende des 20. Jahrhunderts und nach dem Mauerfall gegenüber sahen. Zudem bevorzugt jene Klientel, deren Status und Wohlstand traditionell die Existenz von Luxushotels erklärt, zumeist eher Häuser mit einer zumindest ähnlich langen Geschichte wie jene der eigenen Familie.

Vor diesem Hintergrund kann der Schritt der Betreiber nicht hoch genug geschätzt werden, da hier einmal nicht nostalgisch eine Bildwelt der Vergangenheit evoziert und reproduziert wird. Zugute gekommen ist dem Betreiber dabei gewiß der Standort am Potsdamer Platz. Dieser, doppeldeutig als Filetstück im Herzen der ehemals geteilten Stadt bezeichnet, verdankt dem Genueser Architekten Renzo Piano seinen «Masterplan», in welchen sich der Madrilene Rafael Moneo mit dem Projekt des Grand Hyatt zurückhaltend, und gerade darum meisterlich, eingefügt hat.

Das Grand Hyatt Berlin wirkt von außen zunächst unauffällig, und es ist anzunehmen, daß dem keinesfalls zufällig so ist. Luxus kann, spätestens seit Adolf Loos, eben kaum mehr in opulenter Äußerlichkeit bestehen. Insofern auch war nur konsequent, wenn Rafael Moneo sich mit seinem Partner, dem Wahl-Zürcher Hannes Wettstein, bei der Raumgestaltung darauf konzentriert hat, dem Gast zu einer Rückzugsinsel zu verhelfen, die ihre Qualitäten erst im Bezug (des Zimmers, der Suite) offenbart.

So ist die Lobby eine Ruheinsel, die abschirmt gegen die Hektik der Außenwelt und die zugleich, wie es ein Journalist spontan vor Ort formuliert hat, etwas von der Weltläufigkeit jener Metropolen erahnen läßt, die Berlin mehr als fünfundsiebzig Jahre – zumal an diesem Platz – gefehlt hat. Ferner haben Hannes Wettstein und Rafael Moneo dem architektonischen Layout des Hotels durch weitreichende Synchronisation eine raumgestaltende Handschrift hinzugefügt, die sich eben nicht – wie für «Designer-» (oder sogenannte Boutique-) Hotels üblich – auf den schönen Schein der Oberflächlichkeit beschränkt.

Tatsächlich wurde im Grand Hyatt Berlin vermutbaren ziselierten (Kaschier-)Leisten oder Brokaten eine materialgerechte Sachlichkeit gegenübergestellt, die allenfalls in völliger Unkenntnis der Architekturgeschichte als nüchtern zu bezeichnen wäre. So sind etwa Hölzer und roter Teppich zugleich eindeutig, aber unaufdringlich; Signum und Referenz an das Grand Hotel der Belle Epoque. Zudem sind Annehmlichkeiten postmoderner Nomaden (vom Bad über Minibar mit Teekocher bis zum Telefon und TV) hier zum maßgeblichen Bestandteil einer raumgestaltenden und prägenden Konzeption geworden.

Ebensolches läßt sich zur Kunst feststellen, die von Hannes Wettstein in ihrem Potential als prägnantes Gestaltungselement erkannt und definiert worden ist. Während aber draußen mit Keith Haring, Nam June Paik und Robert Rauschenberg international bekannte Namen dominieren, herrschen im Hotel Bezüge zu Ort und Sprachraum vor. So reflektiert etwa die Bauhaus-Photographie in den Standardzimmern die Geschichte der weltberühmten Institution (wie sie auch mit Walter Benjamins Idee des Kunstwerks im Zeitalter seiner technischen Reproduzierbarkeit spielt). In den exklusiveren Suiten und in den Sonderbereichen (Lobby, Restaurant «Tizian» im Erdgeschoß; Boardroom und Library im ersten Obergeschoß; Regency-Club und Spa im siebten und achten OG) beziehen sich Originale mal bekannterer, mal weniger bekannter Künstler auf Bedingungen des Raums oder – abstrakter – auf dessen atmosphärische Bedingungen.

All das wäre in der dargebotenen Konsequenz kaum möglich ohne das außergewöhnliche Engagement aller Beteiligten. Es wäre zudem kaum möglich geworden, als hier die zeitlichen Rahmenbedingungen seiner Entstehung mehr als einmal gegen das jetzt sichtbare Ergebnis zu sprechen schienen. Insofern und vor allem gilt ein ganz besonderer Dank

dem Bauherrn, der Hyatt Corporation und dort namentlich Bernd Chorengel. Dank gebührt aber auch dem Investor, der Daimler Chrysler Immobiliengesellschaft. Und nicht zuletzt ist es dem Team von Sophie Ott (Schwerpunkt: «Sonderbereiche/Suiten») zu danken, wenn ein anspruchsvolles Kunstkonzept realisiert werden konnte, welches jedoch ohne die Expertise von Hans J. Baumgart (Daimler Chrysler Kunstbesitz; Schwerpunkt «Öffentliche Bereiche») so nie zustande gekommen wäre.

Nicht vergessen werden sollte in diesem Zusammenhang auch, daß jedes Bauwerk immer erst in der Summe ungezählter Gewerke zu einem Ganzen wird. Darüber werden all die kleinen Wunder, die Handwerkerscharen auf einer Baustelle tagtäglich vollbringen, nur allzu oft und allzu gern vergessen und verschwiegen. All jenen sei wenigstens auf diesem Weg ein Wort respektvollen Danks als Zeichen der Anerkennung nachgereicht!

Der Dank an Rafael Moneo und Hannes Wettstein, als jenen, ohne deren gestalterische Vision und Kraft es dieses Buch schließlich gar nicht geben könnte, sollte – zumindest längerfristig – ohnehin weniger in gedruckten Lobeshymnen bestehen, als vielmehr in einer Klientel, die dieses Hotel in seiner Eigenständigkeit zu schätzen weiß. Und wären darunter auch nur wenige, die das Grand Hyatt Berlin wegen dieser eigenständigen Atmosphäre und außergewöhnlichen Details weiterempfehlen, so stünde es vielleicht irgendwann in der Zukunft exemplarisch für eine überfällige Neu-Orientierung einer Branche, die sich «Gastlichkeit» auf die Fahnen geschrieben hat und dabei diese zu sehr losgelöst von ihren räumlichen Bedingungen betrachtet.

Verließ sich diese Branche doch bisher nur allzu gern auf die Marktforschung. Die jedoch muß zwangsläufig zur Bestätigung bereits bewährter Erkenntnisse tendieren, als sie kaum demoskopisch zukünftigen Chancen vorgreifen kann. Oder, wie es der Hyatt-Marketing-Chef Alan Edgar einmal ausgedrückt hat: «...Das Problem mit dem Markt ist: wenn man nur ihn gefragt hätte, dann wäre der Sony-Walkman nie erfunden worden. Es brauchte Sony, um den Markt zu führen.»

In diesem Sinne steht zu hoffen, daß diese Dokumentation des Grand Hyatt Berlin nicht nur Architekten, Kunst-Schaffenden und Raumgestaltern als anregender Fundus dient. Denn erst wenn auch unter den Entscheidern zunehmend Projekte dieser Art als Chance begriffen werden, erhalten Orte das, was ehedem Grand-Hotels, wie etwa jenen eines Cäsar Ritz, zu ihrer bis heute magnetisch anziehenden Geschichte verhalf: Kultur und Geschichte sind eben kein Besitz, den man einfach im Rücken hat. Sie bleiben vielmehr nur dann am leben, wenn sie als Fundus der Innovation begriffen und immer wieder neu verarbeitet werden. Oder, noch einmal mit den Worten von Alan Edgar: «Inzwischen hat das Hyatt Berlin bereits viele Gäste, die das Ganze lieben.» Ein höheres Maß der Anerkennung kann es für den Mut zum Neuen eigentlich kaum geben!

metropolises, a cosmopolitanism that Berlin has lacked for more than seventy-five years now. Furthermore, by attaining a considerable degree of synchronisation in their interior design, Hannes Wettstein and Rafael Moneo have put their own personal stamp on the architectural layout of the hotel, refusing to restrict themselves to the pretty surface illusions so typical of 'designer' (or so-called boutique) hotels.

Indeed, at the Grand Hyatt Berlin, there is none of the ornamental moulding or brocades one might normally expect. Instead, the design reflects a rational approach showing respect for the materials, however only someone unfamiliar with the history of architecture would describe it as sober. Hence, the woods used and the red carpet are both unambiguous and discreet: a signum of and allusion to the grand hotel of the belle époque. Moreover, in this approach, the conveniences and comforts of the post-modernist nomad (bath, minibar with teamaker, telephone, TV, etc.) have become the key elements in a concept that both defines and designs interior space at the same time.

The same applies to the art, whose potential Hannes Wettstein has recognised and defined as a pithy design element. Whereas names of international renown predominate on the outside, e.g. Keith Haring, Nam June Paik and Robert Rauschenberg, references to the location and the cultural heritage preponderate inside the hotel. Thus, for instance, the Bauhaus photographs in the standard rooms reflect the history of that world-famous institution (just as they play with Walter Benjamin's idea of the work of art

in the era of mechanical reproduction). In the more exclusive suites and special areas (the lobby, the Tizian restaurant on the ground floor; the boardroom and the library on the first floor; the Regency Club and the spa on the seventh and eighth floors), originals painted by more famous and by less known artists relate to the rooms or – at a more abstract level – to their atmospheric conditions.

It would have been almost impossible to achieve such a degree of consistency without the extraordinary commitment of everyone involved. And there were many occasions when it seemed as if the stipulated time schedule alone would prevent the realisation of the result now before us. Consequently, our special thanks are due, above all, to the client, the Hyatt Corporation, and to Hyatt's Bernd Chorengel. Our thanks also go to the investor, the Daimler Chrysler Immobiliengesellschäft, and last but not least, to the team around Sophie Ott (main field of activity: special areas/suites), who, aided by the expertise of Hans J. Baumgart Daimler Chrysler art collection (main field of activity: public areas), made the realisation of this ambitious art concept possible.

However, we should not forget that a work of architecture can only ever become a whole as the sum of the countless crafts and trades involved in its completion. All those minor miracles that countless craftsmen perform day in, day out on the site are all too often and all too easily forgotten and passed over. Here, at least, let us extend a word of respectful gratitude to them in acknowledgement of all they have done.

The gratitude shown to Rafael Moneo and Hannes Wettstein, without whose visionary designs and energy this book could never have come into being, ought to be expressed (in the long run at least) less in hymns of praise set down in print, and more in the form of a clientele that shows its appreciation of this hotel as a unique entity. And even if only a few of those guests were to recommend the Grand Hyatt Berlin for its extraordinary atmosphere and remarkable details, the hotel might, some time in the future, stand for a long-overdue reorientation: one that raises the banner of hospitality and recognises that this very hospitality has become divorced from its preconditions: the rooms welcoming its guests.

In the past, the hotel sector has been too quick to rely on market research, which is bound to confirm tried-and-tested ideas, since it is almost impossible to anticipate future openings with demographic means. Or, as Hyatt's marketing manager Alan Edgar once put it: "The problem with the market surveys is that if one had consulted the market alone, the Sony Walkman would never have been invented. It needed Sony to lead the market."

In this sense, one can only hope that the present work on the Grand Hyatt Berlin will be more than a source of inspiration to architects, artists and interior designers. For only when projects of this nature are increasingly seen by decision-makers as an opportunity worth seizing, will those very qualities be restored to urban locations that have always lent grand hotels – like those of a Cäsar Ritz – such a magnetic attraction throughout their history: culture and history, which are certainly not possessions one can fall back

on at will. Rather, they remain alive only if they are grasped as a source of inspiration to be embraced, revised and worked on again and again. Or to quote Alan Edgar again: "The Hyatt Berlin has already found plenty of guests who love it." It will be hard to find a greater degree of recognition for the courage to choose a new path.

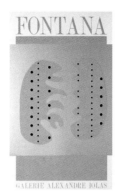

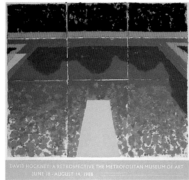

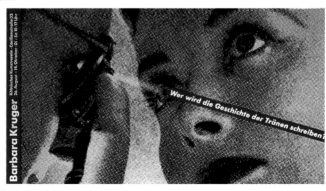

Various posters with different motifs are displayed in the halls, as well as in the mini and single suites.
The selection ranges from the avant-garde of the twenties to contemporary art.

AIDA

Rafael Moneo

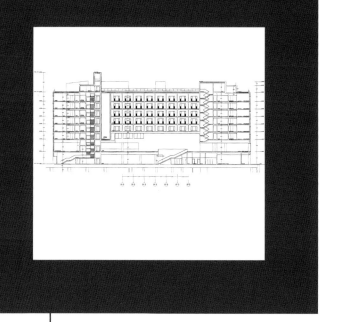

ARCHITECTURE

Rafael Moneo – Ein Spanier in Berlin:
Romantik gegen Rationalismus

Mechthild Heuser

«Lieber Leierkastenmann, fang noch mal von vorne an, deine alten Melodien von der schönen Stadt Berlin...» (aus einem Marlene-Dietrich-Song)

Schon zu Karl Friedrich Schinkels Zeiten war die allseits beklagte preußische Strenge der Garnisonshauptstadt Berlin von dem Geist der Romantik durchtränkt. Während die Soldaten marschierten, blickte Schinkel sehnsüchtig gen Süden, träumte am Wannsee von Neapel und wünschte sich Berlin als Spree-Athen. Heute ist die Stadt ein Aufmarschplatz für Architekten aus aller Welt. Rafael Moneo ist einer unter ihnen. Der gebürtige Spanier wurde unlängst als «last of the Romans» apostrophiert. Dies stimmt nicht nur seiner Herkunft wegen, sondern kennzeichnet ebenso seine Architektur, sofern man «roman» als Kurzform von «Romantic» auffassen möchte.

Betritt man die Hotellobby oder lässt sich in einem der bequemen Ohrensessel nieder, wird man Zeuge eines stummen Dialogs zwischen dem natürlich belichteten gläsernen Kristall, der durch die Decke stößt, und den ihn hinterfangenden, transluzenten Alabastervitrinen. Sie verweisen auf andere Bauten Moneos. Erinnert sei etwa an die Galerie, die er in Palma de Mallorca für die Pilar&Joan Miro Stiftung 1987–92 errichtete. Dort tauchen jene in horizontalen Bändern versetzten, feinädrigen Membranen als Tageslichtblenden, -filter und -weichzeichner zugleich auf, hier stellen sie in ihrer künstlichen Illumination nichts weiter als sich selbst zur Schau. In Berlin erschöpft sich das Zitat im bloßen Dekorum, ist weniger strukturell und funktional bedingter Bestandteil des Gebäudes als vielmehr nachträgliche Zier.

Gläserner Kristall als magische Metapher Berliner Geistes- und Kulturgeschichte
Die Lobby verzichtet auf jeden Bezug zur Außenwelt. Sie gibt sich ganz und gar introvertiert, ja lässt die Welt jenseits der Hotelmauern gar als bedrohlichen Blitzschlag einfahren, wie einen Halleyschen Kometen, der, ohne die Auszugmauern des Planquadrats zu berühren, zielstrebig in das Herz der zweigeschossigen Atriumhalle einschlägt und Geschichte gegenwärtig macht. Geschichte, die hier einst von Baukünstlern erdacht, aber nicht gebaut werden konnte. Assoziationen an die «Gläserne Kette», an Bruno Tauts utopische Visionen von expressionistischen Stadtlandschaften und an Ludwig Mies van der Rohes Phantasien von kristallinen Turmhäusern stellen sich ein. Visionen, die am Potsdamer Platz mit 80jähriger Verspätung endlich Realität geworden sind, in Gestalt der Hochhäuser für Sony und debis.

Angesichts des gläsernen Deckenzapfens schweifen die Gedanken aber auch hinüber, in die Galerie der Romantik des nicht allzu fernen Charlottenburger Schlosses und sammeln sich vor den Bildern Caspar David Friedrichs. Man denkt an seine malerische Beschwörung des berühmten Eismeers, an die Kraft der sich aufbäumenden und übereinander schiebenden Schollen, die das natürliche Gefüge ins Wanken bringen.

Mit dem Rückgewinn all jener magischen Orte, die es an und um den Potsdamer Platz einst gab, entfacht ein Funken Hoffnung neu, der mit dem Naziterror und dem darauffolgenden «antifaschistischen Schutzwall» zu erlöschen drohte: Die Hoffnung auf Geistesblitze, in deren Widerschein die kulturelle Vielfalt der Stadt erneut zu strahlen beginnt.

Rafael Moneo, der bewusst auf einen einheitlichen Stil seiner Bauten verzichtet und dessen Gebäude sich nie kampflos in die bestehende Architektur einfügen, sah sich am Potsdamer Platz einiger Ausdrucksmittel beraubt, derer er sich in jedem anderen Fall ohne Zweifel bedient hätte. Selten drückte die Hypothek fremdbestimmter Baurichtlinien so sehr auf das kreative Potential eines Architekten wie hier. Preußische Disziplin bestimmt die rigide Blockrandbebauung, die Hilmer & Sattler für das gesamte Areal ersonnen haben. Daran konnte auch die nachträgliche Überarbeitung durch Renzo Piano wenig ändern.
Das vorgeschriebene, sklavisch am Straßenverlauf orientierte Blockrandschema raubt dem Baukörper des Grand Hyatt genau jene kristalline Schärfe, die vergleichbare Solitäre Moneos, wie das Veranstaltungszentrum Kursaal in San Sebastian, auszeichnen.

... durch die Hintertür
Die eigentliche und einzige Vorfahrt zum Grand Hyatt befindet sich an der Eichhornstraße. Sie zeigt dem städtischen Treiben am Marlene-Dietrich-Platz und auf der verkehrsberuhigten Alten Potsdamer Straße die kalte Schulter. – Warum gebärdet sich der Haupteingang wie eine Anlieferung?, könnte man fragen. Städtebauliches Konzept und Verkehrsführung ließen keine andere Wahl, lautet die Antwort. Der scheinbare Nachteil birgt infrastrukturelle Vorteile: Film-, Bühnen- und andere Stars wissen die Anonymität der Hintertür durchaus zu schätzen – mit Hilfe eines diskret zugeordneten Nebenfahrstuhls gelangen sie genauso unbemerkt in das Hotel hinein wie anschließend auch wieder hinaus.

Überhaupt besticht die gesamte Infrastruktur dieser Unterkunft der Extraklasse durch gehobene Diskretion. Zwar geleitet ein roter Teppich von der Vorfahrt ins Herz der Hotelhalle hinein, bricht dann aber ohne ersichtlichen Grund vor der >s.15

Above: view of Potsdamer Platz with the new city centre in the background; at the bottom of the picture are the Landwehr Canal and Reichpietschufer, in the centre, the wasteland of a formerly divided city marking the nucleus of the new urban centre at Potsdamer Platz

Oben: Blick auf den Potsdamer Platz mit der neuen Stadtmitte im Bildhintergrund; am unteren Bildrand der Landwehrkanal mit dem Reichpietschufer, in der Bildmitte jene Brache der ehemals geteilten Stadt, die den Kern des Neubau-Areals am Potsdamer Platz markiert

Aerial view of Potsdamer Platz in 1919

Luftaufnahme des Potsdamer Platzes 1919

Potsdamer Platz in 1962

Der Potsdamer Platz 1962

schwarzen Marmorwand einer niedrigeren rückwärtigen Raumnische ab. Ziel verfehlt? Mitnichten. Zur Diskretion gehört auch, Gäste nicht mit der Nase auf jene Dinge zu stoßen, die sie vielleicht lieber nur mit dem Ärmel streifen würden. All die Ziele, an denen in klassischen Hotels kein Weg vorbeiführt, liegen hier am Wegesrand. Dies gilt für die Rezeption ebenso wie für die zentrale Fahrstuhlgruppe oder die «grandes escaliers», als unverzichtbarem Bestandteil jeden Grand-Hotels.

Dieses Grand-Hotel macht seinem Namen zwar was Zimmeranzahl und -komfort angeht alle Ehre, besticht ansonsten aber durch Zurückhaltung. Die ostentativen Mittelpunkte klassischer Hotels rücken hier an die Peripherie. Man kann, muss aber keine Notiz von ihnen nehmen. Wer einen Gast inkognito empfangen möchte, kann diesen ohne allzu große öffentliche Anteilnahme zu sich bitten. Die Anonymität der Großstadt wird auch innerhalb der Hotelmauern zur Kardinaltugend erhoben. Passanten, die sich in der Lobby unter die Gäste mischen sind willkommen, wie und warum sollte man die einen von den anderen unterscheiden? Tatsächlich funktioniert die Lobby wie eine öffentliche Wandelhalle. Man kann sie von einem Eingang zum anderen durchqueren, eines der anliegenden Restaurants oder die Marlene-Bar besuchen, ohne die Hotelfunktion wahr- oder in Anspruch genommen zu haben.

In der Hotelhalle

In dem öffentlichen Erdgeschoss bleibt die Bestimmung des Gebäudes vieldeutig und vage. Ähnlich verhält es sich mit dem Publikum, das sich hier für kurze Zeit niederlässt und zu allerlei Spekulationen Anlass gibt: «Wir saßen in der Halle des großen Hotels, in einer jener Hallen, in denen es immer aussieht wie im Film – … Es war fünf Minuten vor halb sechs; mein Partner war Nervenarzt, seine Sprechstunde war vorüber, und wir tranken einen dünnen Tee. Er war so teuer, dass man schon sagen durfte: wir nahmen den Tee. ‹Sehen Sie›, sagte er, ‹es ist nichts als Übung. Da kommen und gehen sie – Männer und Frauen, Deutsche und Ausländer, Gäste, Besucher … und niemand kennt sie. Ich kenne sie. Ein Blick – … Ich blättere in Leuten wie in aufgeschlagenen Büchern.› ‹Was lesen Sie?› fragte ich ihn. ‹Ganz interessante Kapitelchen.› Er blickt mit zugekniffenen Augen umher. ‹Keine Rätsel hier – ich kenne sie alle. Fragen Sie mich bitte›» – Lesen wir bei Kurt Tucholsky weiter, finden wir vielleicht ähnliche Antworten wie die, die der phantasievolle Herr X dem weniger phantasiebegabten Herrn Y liefert. Ob sie zutreffen, sei nach wie vor dahingestellt. Doch einen Besuch der Lobby des Grand Hyatt wäre die Spekulation allemal wert…

Schwimmen im Himmel über Berlin

Die optische Introvertiertheit der Lobby im Erdgeschoss wird konterkariert durch die Extrovertiertheit des gläsern gewandten Swimmingpools auf dem Dach. Von angenehm warmem Wasser umspielt, sieht man von ferne einen Bruchteil all jener Baudenkmäler älterer und neuerer Zeit panoramatisch an sich vorüberziehen, die man im Laufe des Tages vielleicht noch aus nächster Nähe anschauen möchte. Schwimmen heisst hier, sich zwanglos zwischen Monumenten der älteren und jüngeren Berliner Baugeschichte fortzubewegen: Als Fokus der 25 m Bahn rückt Renzo Pianos debis-Haus in den Blick. Das Durchmessen der Bahn gestaltet sich ähnlich einer Kamerafahrt, Heranzoomen an das debis-Hochhaus und allmähliches Entfernen, vorbei an dem zum Greifen nahen, golden glänzenden Büchersarg der Staatsbibliothek Hans Scharouns, die von ferne grüßende Turmspitze der Matthäikirche streifend, der goldenen Victoria auf der Siegessäule in Gedanken zuzwinkernd, – schwimmend durch das Panorama der Großstadt Berlin. Schinkel hat es seinerzeit (vor 150 Jahren) für die Friedrichstadt vorweggenommen, Rafael Moneo legt die Umgebung des Potsdamer Platzes seinen Hotelgästen zu Füßen.

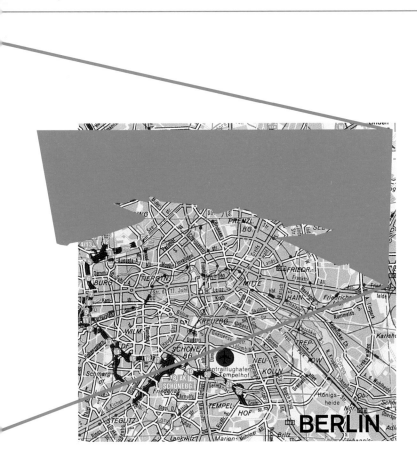

Detail of a map of the site in the city of Berlin

Ausschnitt aus einem Übersichtsplan zur Lage in der Stadt Berlin

For a time it was the biggest building site in Europe: the site under construction

Für einige Zeit die größte Baustelle Europas: Das Areal während der Realisation

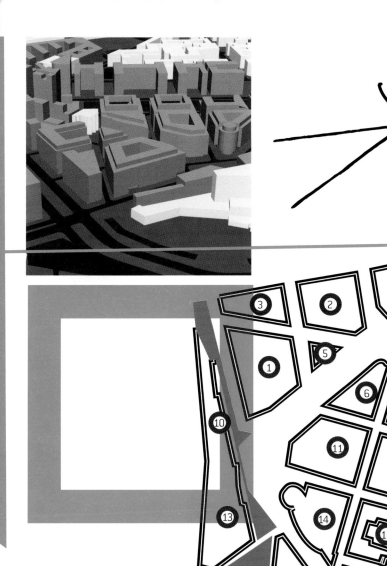

1 Grand Hyatt Hotel
2 Wohnhaus und Cinemaxx Kinocenter
3 Bürohaus
4 Bürohaus
5 Wohnhaus
6 Wohnhaus
7 Bürohaus
8 Weinhaus Huth
9 Bürohaus
10 Spielcasino
11 Wohnhaus
12 Bürohaus
13 Musical-Theater
14 Big Screen 3D-Theater
15 Bürohaus
16 Wohnhaus
17 Bürohaus der Zentrale der Debis und weitere
    Bereiche des Daimler-Benz Konzerns
18/19 Bürohäuser

Computer animation of the area
Computer-Animation des Areals

The masterplan for the Daimler Chrysler site at Potsdamer Platz (1994) and the signet Renzo Piano created from the plan (above)
Der Masterplan für das «Daimler-Chrysler-Areal» am Potsdamer Platz (1994) und das aus diesem Plan von Renzo Piano generierte Signet (oben)

Rafael Moneo – A Spaniard in Berlin: Romantic Style versus Rationalism

Mechthild Heuser

"Oh, hurdy-gurdy man, play your song for me again, your old melodies of the beautiful city of Berlin..." (from a Marlene Dietrich song)

Even at the time of Karl Friedrich Schinkel, the much-bewailed Prussian severity of the garrison city of Berlin was steeped in the spirit of romanticism. Whilst the soldiers were marching, Schinkel looked south, dreaming of Naples as he stood by Wannsee lake in Berlin, longing to see Berlin transformed into an Athens on the river Spree.

Today, the city has become a parade ground for architects from all over the world. Rafael Moneo is one of them. Someone recently described the native of Spain as the "last of the Romans". This is true not only of his origins, but also of his architecture, if one is prepared to consider "Roman" as an abbreviation for "romantic". Entering the hotel lobby or sitting down in one of the comfortable wing-chairs, one becomes witness to a silent dialogue between the two naturally lit glass crystal-shaped pyramids piercing the ceiling, and the translucent alabaster screens on the walls. They are allusions to other buildings by Moneo, such as the gallery he designed for the Pilar & Joan Miro Foundation in Palma de Mallorca in 1987–92.

There, the finely veined membranes set back in horizontal bands assume the form of sun shades, filters and soft-focus lenses; here, artificially illuminated, they stand for themselves alone. In Berlin, the citation exhausts itself in pure decoration, serving less as a structurally and functionally determined component of the building than as added embellishment.

Glass crystal as a magic metaphor of Berlin's intellectual and cultural history

The lobby dispenses with any reference to the outside world. Creating an impression of total introversion, the lobby makes the world beyond the hotel walls appear to enter the building like an ominous flash of lightning, or a Halley's Comet which, without touching the extension wall of the grid square, homes in on the heart of the two-storey atrium, bringing history to life. At one time, history was only conceived by architects here, with no chance of it being realised in constructed form. Associations arise: the "glass necklace", Bruno Taut's utopian visions of expressionist cityscapes and Ludwig Mies van der Rohe's dream of creating all-glass tower blocks. Now – some eighty years on – these visions have finally become reality at Potsdamer Platz in the form of the Sony and debis towers. At the sight of the glass crystal in the ceiling, one's thoughts turn to the works of romantic art on exhibition at the not-too-distant Charlottenburg Palace, where they collect in front of the Caspar David Friedrich paintings hanging there. His famous painting evoking the Arctic Ocean springs to mind: the force behind the ice-floes as they surge upwards, pushing up against one another, shaking the natural order of things to its very foundations. By reclaiming all those magical places that formerly existed in and around Potsdamer Platz, a glimmer of hope has again arisen which was in danger of disappearing forever in the face of Nazi terror and the later "anti-fascist protection wall": the hope of flashes of inspiration in whose reflection the cultural diversity of the city will again start to glow.

Rafael Moneo consciously avoids imposing a uniform style on his buildings, which never simply adapt to the surrounding architecture without first putting up a struggle. At Potsdamer Platz, he found himself deprived of diverse means of expression that he would have undoubtedly drawn upon under any other circumstances. The burden of building directives dictated by others has seldom weighed so heavily on the creative potential of an architect as it has here. Prussian discipline demanded rigid adherence to the street blocks, following a plan devised by Hilmer & Sattler for the entire site. Nor did Renzo Piano's subsequent revisions significantly change this state of affairs. The prescribed block plan, which slavishly followed the course of the streets, deprived the Grand Hyatt building of that very crystalline sharpness which distinguishes similar solitary structures by Rafael Moneo, such as the Kursaal Auditorium and Congress Centre in San Sebastian.

Entering by the back door

The only driveway to the Grand Hyatt is in Eichhornstrasse. It turns a cold shoulder to the bustling city life at Marlene-Dietrich-Platz and on the traffic-calmed Alte Potsdamer Strasse. One is tempted to ask why the main entrance poses as a delivery entrance.

The answer? – The urban-planning concept and traffic routes allowed no other choice. But this apparent disadvantage has its advantages: stars of the screen, the stage and other fields well >p.20

The façade of the Grand Hyatt Berlin showing the entrance area. The debis building (architecture: Renzo Piano) is in the background

Die Fassade des Grand Hyatt Berlin mit dem Eingangsbereich; im Hintergrund die Gebäude der «debis» (Architektur: Renzo Piano)

appreciate the anonymity of the back-door. Using a discreetly located secondary lift they can enter the hotel as unnoticed as they can leave it later. In any case, the entire infrastructure of this first-class hotel enchants visitors by its refined discretion. Although a red carpet takes visitors from the driveway into the very heart of the lobby, it suddenly stops for no apparent reason in front of the black marble wall separating a low niche at the back. A faux pas? Certainly not. Discretion also means not feeling a need to spell everything out to the guests, but letting them discover things in their own good time. All those elements that are so self-evident in the classical hotel have been shifted to the periphery here. This is as true for the reception as it is for the central lift group and the "grandes escaliers", an indispensable component in any grand hotel.

Whilst this grand hotel certainly does great credit to its name in terms of room numbers and comfort, its captivating quality lies in its demureness. The ostentatious focal points of the classical hotel are relegated to the background here. One can take note of them, but there is no obligation to do so. Anyone who wants to receive a guest incognito can do so without attracting too much public attention. The anonymity of the city is raised to the status of a cardinal virtue within the hotel walls.

Passers-by are welcome to come in and mingle with the guests in the lobby; how and why should one make distinctions between them? In fact, the lobby serves as a public foyer. People can cross it from one entrance to the other, visit one of the adjacent restaurants or pop into the Marlene Bar without taking note of or using any of the hotel functions.

In the hotel lobby

On the public ground floor, the building's purpose is ambiguous and vague. Nor is the situation so very different for members of the public who briefly rest here, giving cause for all kinds of speculation: "We sat in the lobby of the big hotel, in one of those lobbies which always look like they do in films – ... It was twenty-five past five, my partner was a neurologist, his surgery hours were over and we stopped for a cup of rather weak tea. It was so expensive that one could have justifiably said: we took tea. 'You see,' he said, 'it is merely a question of practice. They come and go – men and women, Germans and foreigners, guests, visitors... and nobody knows them. I know them. A glance – I browse through people the way I do open books.' 'What can you read there?' I ask him. 'Fascinating little chapters.' He looks around, his eyes squinting. 'Nothing mysterious about them – I know them all. Just ask me.'" If we continued reading Kurt Tucholsky we might find similar answers to those that an imaginative Mr. X gives to a less imaginative Mr. Y. Whether they apply or not remains an open question. However, a visit to the Grand Hyatt would certainly be worth it for the speculation alone...

Swimming in the sky above Berlin

The introverted impression made by the lobby on the ground floor is counteracted by the extroverted character of the glass-clad swimming pool on the roof.

Completely surrounded by warm, pleasant, lapping water, one can see from afar a fragment of all of those monuments and old buildings from both the distant and more recent past in a vast panorama: fragments that one might feel like seeing at close range during the course of the day.

In this context, swimming means moving effortlessly between the monuments of Berlin's past and more recent architectural history. The focal point of the 25 m lane, Renzo Piano's debis building, comes into view. Completing the lane, one is reminded of the travelling of a camera: zooming in on the debis tower and gradually retreating, passing almost within reach of Hans Scharoun's shining-gold book-coffin, the State Library; barely touching the spire of St. Mathew's Church extending its greetings from afar; mentally waving to the gold statue of Victoria crowning the Victory Column - swimming through the panorama presented by the city of Berlin. In his day (150 years ago), Schinkel anticipated this move in Friedrichstadt; now Rafael Moneo has laid the surroundings of Potsdamer Platz at the feet of his hotel guests.

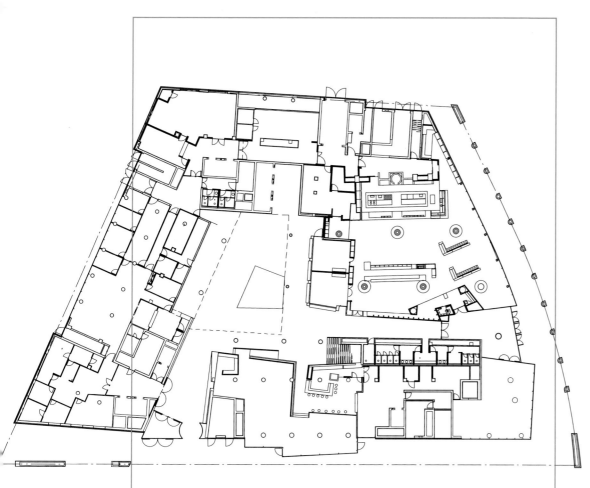

Ground Floor

Ground floor plan
Grundrißplan EG (Erdgeschoß)

View of the corner by Marlene-Dietrich-Platz with the Dietrich Bistro (arch. Dani Freixes, Barcelona)

Blick auf die Ecke am Marlene-Dietrich-Platz mit dem Bistro «Dietrich» (Arch. Dani Freixes, Barcelona)

The arcades in front of the Vox restaurant at Alte Potsdamer Strasse

Die Arkaden vor dem «Vox»-Restaurant zur Alten Potsdamer Straße

View into the lobby: in the foreground a work by the artist John Armleder, with reception in the background

Blick in die Lobby: im Vordergrund eine Arbeit des Künstlers John Armleder, im Hintergrund die Rezeption

View of the entrance from the lobby (art: John Armleder): elements of the group of seats in the foreground (design: Hannes Wettstein)

Blick aus der Lobby auf den Eingang (Kunst: John Armleder): im Vordergrund Elemente der Sitzgruppe (Design: Hannes Wettstein)

The lobby from a worm's-eye-view: at the end of the red carpet, two works by the artist Ingrid Hartlieb (*Buoys*), above them the artwork *ready mix (a) 1* by Gerold Miller

Die Hotel-Lobby aus der Froschperspektive: am Ende des roten Teppichs zwei Arbeiten der Künstlerin Ingrid Hartlieb («Bojen»), darüber die Arbeit «ready mix (a) 1» von Gerold Miller

The stairs to the ballrooms and conference rooms
Der Aufgang zu den Ballsälen und Konferenzräumen

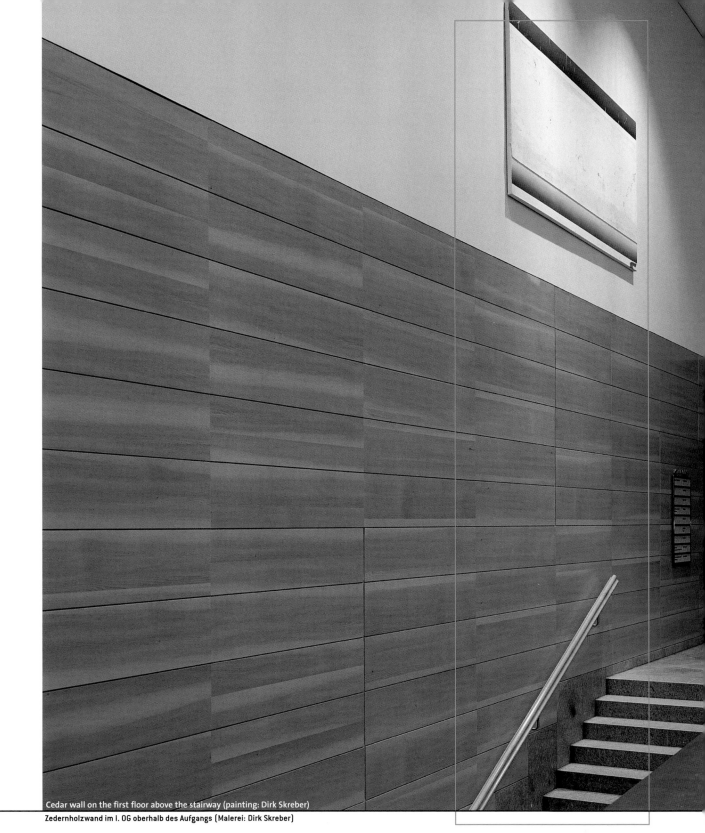

Cedar wall on the first floor above the stairway (painting: Dirk Skreber)

Zedernholzwand im I. OG oberhalb des Aufgangs (Malerei: Dirk Skreber)

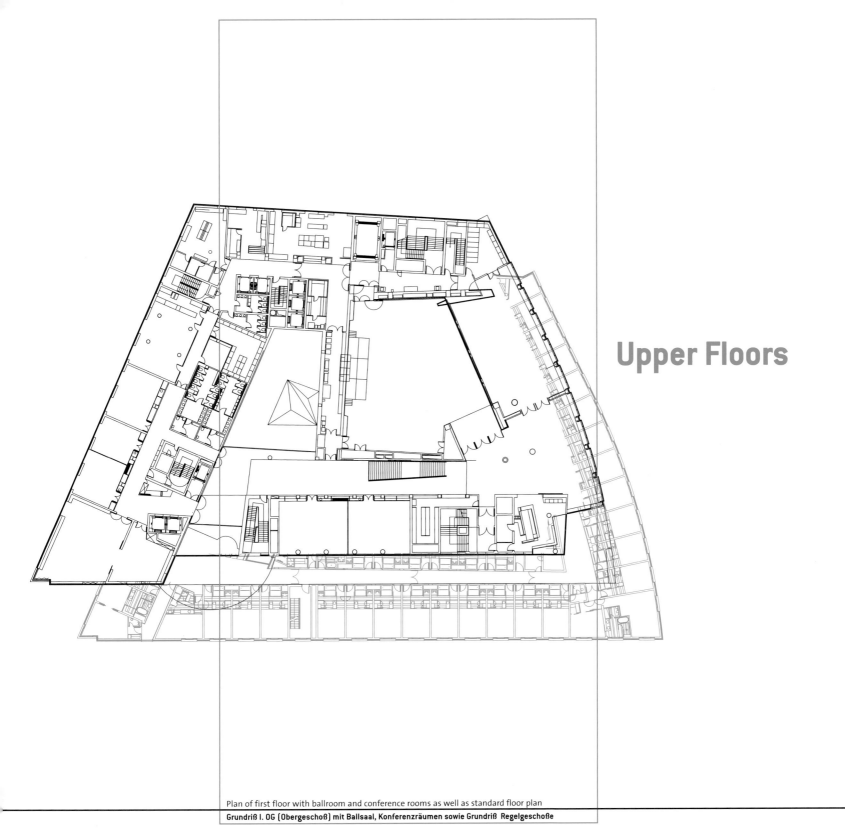

Upper Floors

Plan of first floor with ballroom and conference rooms as well as standard floor plan

Grundriß I. OG (Obergeschoß) mit Ballsaal, Konferenzräumen sowie Grundriß Regelgeschoße

First floor: view of the wall drawing by the artist Otto Zitko above the entrance to the boardroom / library and conference rooms
I. OG: Blick auf die Wandzeichnung des Künstlers Otto Zitko oberhalb des Durchgangs zu «Boardroom / Library» u.a. Konferenzräume

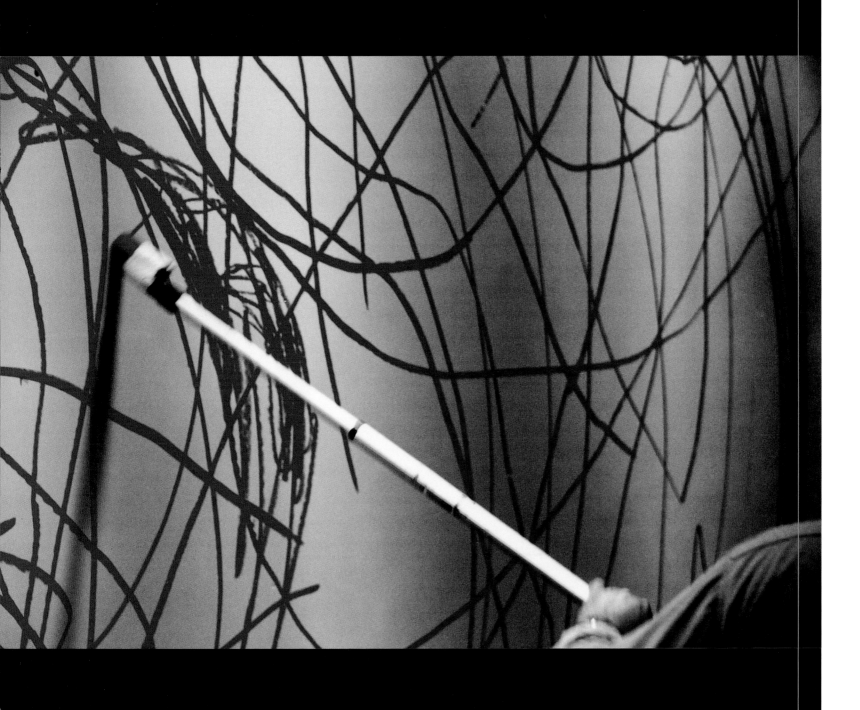

"Work in progress": Otto Zitko executing his wall drawing
«Work in progress»: Otto Zitko beim Be-Zeichnen der Wand

Corridors in the standard floors (2 to 6); waiting zone in front of the lifts (plinth with sculpture by Jo Schöpfer)

Flure der «Regel»-Geschoße (II bis VI); Wartezone vor den Aufzügen (Sockel mit Plastik von Jo Schöpfer)

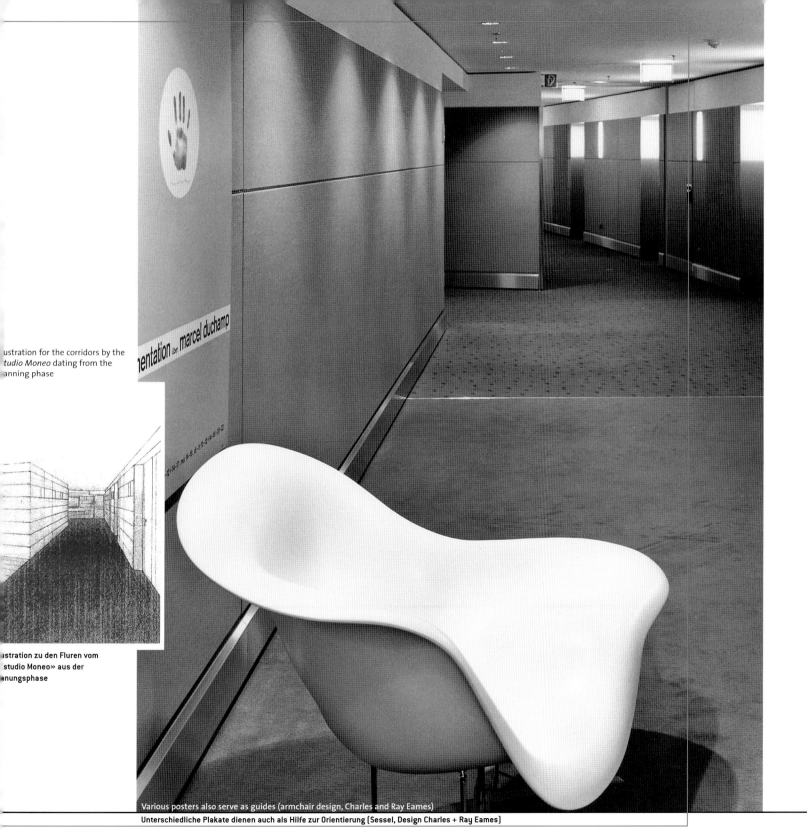

istration for the corridors by the
tudio Moneo dating from the
anning phase

istration zu den Fluren vom
«studio Moneo» aus der
anungsphase

Various posters also serve as guides (armchair design, Charles and Ray Eames)

Unterschiedliche Plakate dienen auch als Hilfe zur Orientierung (Sessel, Design Charles + Ray Eames)

Close-up from the rest area (Wellness area) on the 8th floor; Red-Blue-Yellow triptych by Gert Rappenecker

Ausschnitt aus der Ruhezone in der VIII. Etage («Wellnes»-Bereich); rot-blau-gelbes Triptychon von Gert Rappenecker

Top Floor

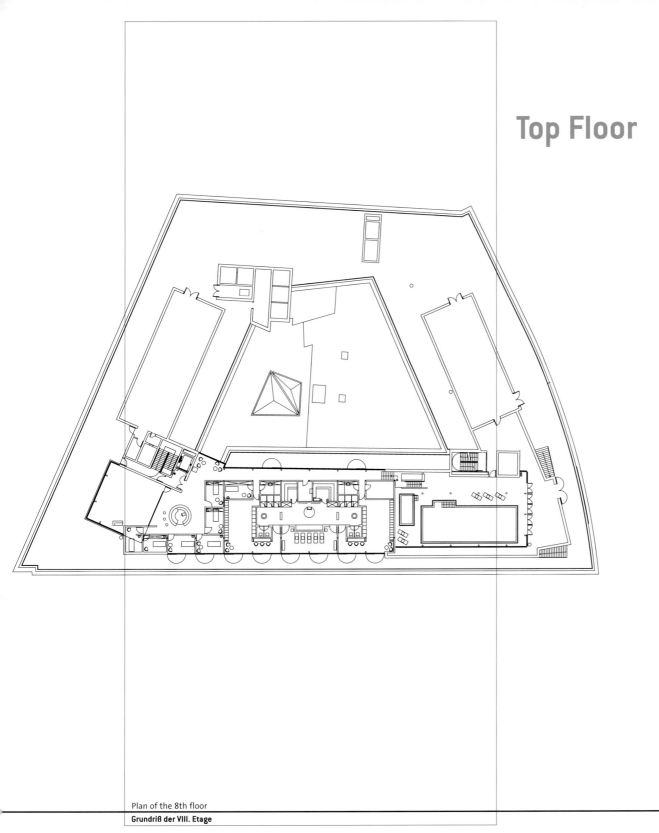

Plan of the 8th floor
Grundriß der VIII. Etage

The Swimming pool above the roofs of Berlin

Blick auf den «Swimmingpool» über den Dächern von Berlin

The stream shower and the cold bath in the wet area of the spa

Die Schwalldusche und das Kaltbad im Nassbereich des Spa

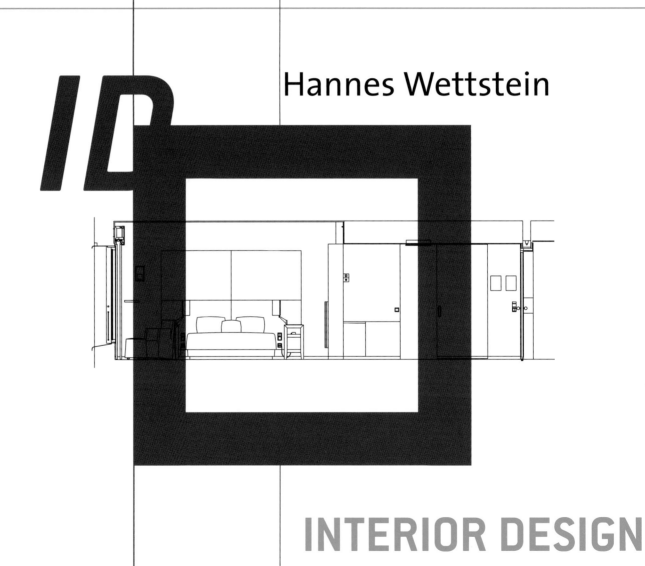

Hannes Wettstein

INTERIOR DESIGN

Integration statt Addition

Hubertus Adam

Hannes Wettstein definiert ein Hotel der Fünf-Sterne-Kategorie neu

Die wenigsten Gäste übernachten heutzutage freiwillig in einem Hotel. Mal bedarf der kurzfristigen Bleibe zwischen zwei Geschäftsterminen in einer fremden Stadt, dann wieder ist die Wohnung der Freunde zu klein oder gerade besetzt: im Zeitalter der Mobilität gilt das Hotel nicht als eigentliches Ziel der Reise. Das tatsächliche Leben findet anderenorts statt; die Institution Hotel hat ihren öffentlichen Charakter verloren und sich auf regenerative Funktionen reduzieren lassen.

Das war nicht immer so. Zu Beginn des Jahrhunderts galt der – mitunter mehrwöchige – Aufenthalt im Grand Hotel als gesellschaftliches Ereignis; in den Ball- und Speisesälen träumte die Bourgeoisie von anderen, von vermeintlich besseren Zeiten, spielte noch einmal Aristokratie. Die Zeiten wandelten sich, die Bourgeoisie wurde zum bürgerlichen Mittelstand, doch die Hotelhalle, wo kurz zuvor noch der Geist des Ancien Régime geherrscht hatte, blieb ein magischer Ort der Voyeure und Akteure, Laufsteg und Schaubühne zugleich.

In der zweiten Hälfte des 20. Jahrhunderts mutierte das Hotel zum Beherbergungsbetrieb, dessen einziger Zweck darin bestand, den sich tagsüber anderenorts verausgabenden Gästen die Gelegenheit zu physischer Regeneration zu geben. Die Zeiten von Glanz und Glamour waren unwiederbringlich vorbei, an die Stelle der einstigen magischen Paläste traten die gesichtslosen Bettenburgen der Spätmoderne, die konfektionierten Kettenhotels mit ihrer sterilen, auf die angeblichen Bedürfnisse von Geschäftsreisenden zugeschnittenen Ausstattung.

Seit Mitte der Achtzigerjahre scheint dieser Trend gebrochen, zumindest relativiert – 1985 eröffnete Ian Schrager in Manhattan das «Morgans», dessen distinguierte Möblierung und Ausstattung durch die Pariser Gestalterin Andrée Putman neue Maßstäbe setzte. Die Idee des Designhotels war geboren; Hotelmanager entdeckten, dass Namen wie Putman oder Philippe Starck in einer designorientierten Ära für manche Menschen Grund genug sind, ein Hotel aufzusuchen – die Übernachtung wird im Verständnis der Gäste zum kulturellen Event, der ästhetische Mehrwert legitimiert höhere Preise. Schragers jüngster Coup, mit Rem Koolhaas sowie Herzog & de Meuron zwei der derzeit renommiertesten Architekturbüros für ein Hotel in Downtown Manhattan zusammenzuspannen, belegt, wie sehr man sich der Zugkraft von Stararchitektur bewusst ist. Und der agile Luzerner Hotelier Urs Karli eröffnete sein von Jean Nouvel eingerichtetes Hotel beinahe zeitgleich mit der Gesamteinweihung des in unmittelbarer Nachbarschaft gelegenen Kultur- und Kongresszentrums Luzern, das inzwischen unzweifelhaft als Chefd'œuvre des französischen Stararchitekten gilt.

Der Siegeszug der Kunst- und Designhotels dürfte nicht zuletzt durch einen gesamtgesellschaftlichen Trend zu einem ausgeprägten, unverwechselbaren Lebensstil befördert werden. Für eine Reihe von Besuchern erweist sich die Qualität eines Hotels nicht mehr allein an Service und Standard; entscheidend wird zunehmend der Faktor der Individualität und Authentizität. Gerade Philippe Starck gelang es dank seiner überbordenden Phantasie, Sinnlichkeit zurückzugewinnen. Dabei entlädt sich seine Ideenvielfalt nicht in planlosem Formenüberschwang, sondern generierte eine präzise kalkulierte Abfolge von Bildern – Bildern der Opulenz, aber auch Bildern leiser Melancholie, die Hotels als Orten des Transitorischen anhaftet.

Wenn jedoch – wie in den Häusern der Gruppe «art'otel» – Kunst und Design nachträgliche Dekoration schon vorher entworfener Gebäude darstellen, wirkt das Resultat selten ansprechend. Eine Massierung an Gestaltung triumphiert hier über Qualität, das Konzept zeugt von dem Irrglauben der Verantwortlichen, man müsse nur was Rang und Namen hat kombinieren, und schon stelle sich der Erfolg von selbst ein. Projekte wie jenes des Kunsthotels «Teufelhof» in Basel oder das von Nouvels «The Hotel» in Luzern mit seinen insgesamt 25 Zimmern und Suiten beweisen, dass sich anspruchsvolle Konzepte eher in kleinem Maßstab durchsetzen lassen – und überdies dringend des vorbehaltlosen Engagements einer individuellen Hotelierpersönlichkeit bedürfen.

Das Management international agierender Hotelketten, zumeist im Vorurteil befangen, ein Hotelzimmer müsse in New York, Berlin oder Barcelona gleich aussehen (das heisst: gleich langweilig), zeigt sich ambitionierten gestalterischen Konzepten gegenüber selten aufgeschlossen. Dass es Rafael Moneo und Hannes Wettstein mit dem Grand Hyatt Berlin am Potsdamer Platz gelungen ist, ein Hotel der Fünf-Sterne-Kategorie jenseits von stereotyper Tristesse oder plüschiger Verschmocktheit neu zu definieren, mutet unter diesen Rahmenbedingungen wie ein kleines Wunder an. Noch mehr erstaunt das Ergebnis, bedenkt man, dass Architekt und Designer in diesem Fall nicht nur dem ökonomischen Druck des Investors sowie dem ausgeklügelten Raumprogramm des Betreibers ausgesetzt waren, sondern überdies städtebaulichen Richtlinien, die der Bauaufgabe Luxushotel nicht eben auf den Leib geschneidert waren. Wo gemeinhin ein ausladender Sockelbereich mit einem darüber sich erhebenden Bettenriegel errichtet wird, sahen sich die Planer hier mit der Maßgabe einer trapezoiden, die traditionelle Berliner Traufkante respektierenden Blockrandstruktur konfrontiert. Moneo und Wettstein haben indes aus der Not des unregelmässigen Grundrisses eine Tugend gemacht: in den für Standardzimmer schwer nutzbaren spitzen und stumpfen Ecken wurden die Suiten angeordnet, die somit schon allein durch ihre Grundrisse ein außergewöhnliches Raumerlebnis garantieren; die ringförmig verbundenen Flure ließen sich vor den Aufzügen weiten und somit in eine – auch durch das Dessin des Teppichbodens unterstützte – Sequenz aus intimeren und öffentlicheren Bereichen differenzieren. >s.43

Integration not addition

Hubertus Adam

Hannes Wettstein redefines the five-star hotel

Few people would choose to spend the night in a hotel nowadays.

But then, one evening, you suddenly need a place to stay in a strange town between two business appointments; another time a friend's apartment is either too small or happens to be full that particular night. In an age of mobility, travellers no longer see the hotel itself as their destination. Real life takes place elsewhere. The hotel, having lost its public character as an institution, has been reduced to its purely regenerative functions.

It hasn't always been this way. In the early 1900s, a stay in a grand hotel, sometimes lasting anything up to several weeks at a time, was considered a social event; in the ballrooms and dining halls, the bourgeoisie dreamed of different and ostensibly better times, playing the part of the aristocracy one last time. Then the times changed, and the bourgeoisie became the middle class; but the hotel lobby, where the spirit of the ancien régime had prevailed only a short time before, retained its magical charm for voyeurs and actors, for the catwalk and the theatre. In the second half of the twentieth century, the hotel mutated into an accommodation enterprise whose sole purpose was to provide a place where guests could recuperate physically after they had exhausted themselves elsewhere. The days of glamour and splendour had irrevocably passed, the magical palaces of yesteryear gave way to the gigantic faceless hotels of late Modernism, and to the mass-produced chain hotels with their sterile furnishings tailored to meet the alleged needs of travelling businesspeople.

This trend was apparently interrupted during the mid-eighties, or has at least ceased to predominate. In 1985, Ian Schrager opened Morgan's Hotel in Manhattan. The hotel's distinguished furnishings and fittings, designed by Adrée Putman of Paris, set new standards. The idea of the design hotel was born; hotel managers soon discovered that, in a design-oriented age, names like Putman and Philippe Starck were reason enough for many people to stay at a hotel. For the guests, an overnight stay became a cultural event, the aesthetic added value legitimating the higher prices. Schrager's latest coup (staged with the help of Rem Koolhaas and Herzog & de Meuron) to combine the forces of two of the currently most renowned architects' offices in designing a hotel in downtown Manhattan, shows how conscious people have become of the allure of architecture designed by the stars in the trade. And Urs Karli, the sharp-minded hotelier from Lucerne, opened his hotel, fitted out by Jean Nouvel, at the very same time as the Lucerne Cultural and Congress Centre was being opened nearby, a complex meanwhile considered to be the unchallenged chef-d'oeuvre of the star architect from France.

Thanks, not least to a general social trend, the triumphal progress of art and design hotels is likely to shape a distinct and unmistakable lifestyle. For many visitors, the quality of a hotel no longer depends on services and standards alone; rather, the decisive features are now those of individuality and authenticity. With an exuberant mind teaming with ideas, Philippe Starck, of all people, has succeeded in reclaiming sensuousness. And his fertile imagination did not explode into a chaotic effusion of forms, but generated a precisely calculated sequence of images: images of opulence as well as of a demure melancholy so often associated with hotels as places of transition.

When, however, art and design represent the belated decoration of buildings designed earlier – as is the case with those of the "art hotel" group – we rarely find the result appealing. There, the massing of design ideas triumphs over quality; the concept reflects the misconception on the part of those responsible, that you only have to bring together everybody who is anybody and success is guaranteed automatically. Projects like that of the Teufelhof art hotel (with individual artists exhibiting and designing the different rooms) in Basel, and Nouvel's The Hotel in Lucerne (which has a total of twenty-five rooms and suites), show that quality concepts are more easily realised on a small scale – and, furthermore, that they urgently require the unconditional commitment of an hotelier with a powerful personality.

The managers of internationally operating hotel chains, who usually labour under the misconception that a hotel rooms have to look the same (i.e. equally boring) no matter whether they are located in New York, Berlin or Barcelona, are seldom receptive to ambitious design concepts. The fact that Rafael Moneo and Hannes Wettstein have succeeded, with the Grand Hyatt Berlin at Potsdamer Platz, in creating a new definition of a five-star hotel that goes beyond stereotypical gloom or plush superficiality is nothing short of a miracle under the circumstances. The result is all the more surprising when one recalls that both architect and designer were not only

under economic pressure from the investor, and bound to the sophisticated room concept of the operator, but also restricted by urban-planning directives hardly tailored to meet the task of realising a luxury hotel. Normally, a prominent plinth is erected to form the base of a monolithic hotel rising from it, here, however, the planners faced the task of filling a trapezoidal block whilst respecting the traditional Berlin eaves moulding. Undaunted by this prospect, Moneo and Wittgenstein made a virtue out of the necessity dictated by the irregular ground plan. The suites have been arranged in the acute and obtuse corners, which would have been most unsuitable for standard rooms, thus guaranteeing a very unusual experience of space owing to their plan alone. The ring-shaped corridors linking the rooms were widened at the lifts to form a differentiated sequence – accentuated by the carpet design – of areas with an alternately intimate and public character.

Wettstein accepted the directives: the prime task of a five-star hotel with 300 rooms and 41 suites is to function. Absolute priority must be attached to the efficiency of the services. Given the number of rooms, even the slightest shortcomings can turn into huge – financial – problems.

Even though the lobby and the public areas provide the first impression a hotel makes on its guests, its true quality only really becomes apparent in the furnishings and arrangement of the rooms. This has become particularly true as a result of the total reversal of the relationship between public and private spheres from the end of the nineteenth century on. Whereas a hotel visit used to be a social event, it is now a controlled retreat into temporary intimacy. Hence, all the more attention must be given to the planning of the rooms, which have lost their exclusive status as sleeping cells over the past few decades and have come to serve as entertainment areas and wellness centres, too. This overloading with functions frequently causes designers to capitulate, since they suddenly feel incapable of combining the minibar, television, telephones, beds, cupboards and luggage rack within the framework of a consistent arrangement.

In this context, Hannes Wettstein's room furnishings and fittings are exemplary. Integration, and not the addition of heterogeneous elements, has been his guiding principle. Instead of conceiving bathroom units and bedrooms as completely separate entities he has sought to link them. The hygiene area has been designed as a cube clad in cherry wood; it is positioned in the room so as to separate corridor zone from the lounge and bedroom area. Sliding doors allow the bathroom to be opened on both sides; this not only detracts from the confined character of the hallway situation, but also from the customary hermetic atmosphere of an artificially illuminated bathroom. The high quality of the materialisation, with floors and walls in green marble, a Nero Assoluto granite wash basin, and glass shelves, has made the bathroom into the secret centre of the room. Lingering there means more than simply performing hygienic acts: pushing the wooden wall to one side and standing on the natural stone slabs beneath the shower, installed to permit maximum mobility, the guest has a view across the room and out onto the city. Wettstein has also concealed the wardrobes and lug-gage racks behind an additional sliding wall in the bathroom. This again reveals the interplay between the diverse useful areas. But it also reflects an understanding of design as interior design, representing a departure from the additive principle in favour of a search for architectural form in the interior too. The minibar disappears in the external cladding of the bathroom cube; the television neither hangs from the ceiling like a surveillance camera, nor does it dominate the room like some kind of a cult object that has been placed on a pedestal. Instead, it is integrated into a cupboard continued as a wall panel behind the desk.

There may well be visitors to the Grand Hyatt Berlin who miss excitement in every corner, as they are promised in the hotels designed by Philippe Starck. Those who pursue this line of reasoning fail to appreciate the requirements of a 350-room luxury-class hotel. A building of this nature can hardly be designed for one particular target group alone: it has to accommodate congress visitors as well as cultural tourists, business people, pop stars as well as politicians. This does not mean creating a faceless building, but it does involve a certain degree of neutrality in the interior design. With his carefully considered concept, Hannes Wettstein has created a temporary place of rest in the transitoriness of life. We assume and hope that the guests won't have too much trouble taking care of the excitement themselves. Perhaps they will then appreciate the advantages of living in a hotel after all.

Wettstein akzeptierte die gegebenen Vorgaben: ein Fünf-Sterne-Haus mit 300 Zimmern und 41 Suiten muss zunächst einmal funktionieren. Die Effizienz der Servicevorgänge bleibt oberstes Gebot; selbst kleinste Mängel wachsen sich aufgrund der Anzahl von Räumen zu großen – auch finanziellen – Problemen aus.

Auch wenn Lobby und öffentliche Bereiche den ersten Eindruck des Gasts von einem Hotel bestimmen, erweist sich doch dessen eigentliche Qualität erst an der Einrichtung und Organisation der Zimmer. Dies um so mehr, als sich seit der Jahrhundertwende das Verhältnis von Öffentlichkeit und Privatheit nachgerade umgekehrt hat: war der Besuch eines Hotels früher ein gesellschaftliches Ereignis, so bedeutet er heute den kontrollierten Rückzug in eine temporäre Intimität. Entsprechend mehr Aufmerksamkeit muss bei der Planung den Zimmern zukommen, die in den vergangenen Jahrzehnten ihren alleinigen Status als Schlafzellen verloren haben und nun zugleich als Entertainment Area und Wellness Center fungieren. Diese funktionale Überfrachtung führt häufig zu einer Kapitulation der Gestalter, die nicht mehr vermögen, Minibar, Fernseher, Telefone, Betten, Schränke und Kofferablagen zu einem konsistenten Arrangement zu verbinden.

In diesem Kontext wirkt die Zimmereinrichtung von Hannes Wettstein mustergültig. Nicht Addition des Heterogenen war die Leitlinie, sondern Integration. Anstatt Nasszelle und Schlafraum als zwei voneinander getrennte Einheiten aufzufassen, wird hier die Verbindung gesucht. Der Hygienebereich tritt als kirschholzverkleideter Würfel in Erscheinung, der so in das Zimmer eingestellt ist, dass die Korridorzone vom Aufenthaltsbereich geschieden wird. Schiebetüren erlauben es, das Bad zu beiden Seiten hin zu öffnen; vermieden wird damit nicht nur die Enge der Korridorsituation, sondern auch die übliche Hermetik einer künstlich beleuchteten Nasszelle. Die edle Materialisierung – Boden und Wände aus grünlichem Marmor, Waschtisch aus Granit Nero Assoluto, gläserne Regale – lässt das Bad zum heimlichen Zentrum des Zimmers avancieren. Der Aufenthalt dort bedeutet mehr als die Verrichtung hygienischer Akte; schiebt man die Holzwand beiseite, kann man, auf Natursteinplatten unter der frei im Raum installierten Dusche stehend, durch das Zimmer hindurch auf die Stadt sehen. Überdies hat Wettstein die Kleiderschränke und Kofferablagen hinter einer weiteren verschiebbaren Wand im Bad versteckt. Dies indiziert aufs Neue die Verschränkung der unterschiedlichen Nutzungsbereiche, es steht aber auch für ein Verständnis von Design als Raumgestaltung, für die Abkehr vom additiven Prinzip, für die Suche nach einer architektonischen Form auch im Interieurbereich. Die Minibar verschwindet in der äußeren Verkleidung des Nasszellenwürfels; der Fernseher hängt weder wie eine Überwachungskamera an der Decke, noch ist er wie ein zimmerbeherrschender Kultgegenstand aufgesockelt, sondern wurde in ein Regal integriert, das sich als Wandpaneel hinter dem Arbeitstisch fortsetzt.

Es mag Besucher geben, die vermissen im Grand Hyatt Berlin die Erregung in jeder Zimmerecke, wie sie beispielsweise die Hotels von Philippe Starck versprechen. Wer so argumentiert, verkennt indes die Anforderungen eines 350-Zimmer-Hotels der Luxuskategorie. Ein derartiges Haus lässt sich schwerlich zielgruppenspezifisch ausrichten: es muss die Kongressbesucherin genauso beherbergen wie den Kulturtouristen, die Geschäftsreisende, den Popstar oder die Politikerin. Das erfordert nicht Gesichtslosigkeit, sondern eine gewisse Neutralität in der Raumgestaltung. Hannes Wettstein schafft mit seinem durchdachten Konzept einen temporären Ruhepol in der Transitorik des Lebens. Für die Erregung zu sorgen, so nehmen wir an, so hoffen wir, sollte den Gästen nicht schwer fallen. Und vielleicht weiß man dann doch die Vorzüge des Lebens im Hotel zu schätzen.

Restaurant/Bar

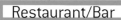

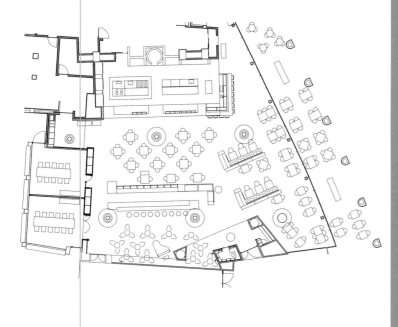

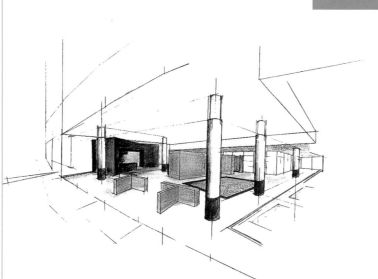

Barman on the first floor (in front of the ballrooms)
Barman im I.OG (vor den Ballsälen)

Plan of the Vox restaurant area on the ground floor of the hotel
Grundriß des Restaurationsbereichs («Vox») im Erdgeschoß des Hotels

Sketch for the colour scheme and material composition of the restaurant
Skizze zur Farb- und Materialkomposition des Restaurants

Detail of the Jazz Bar area of the restaurant
Ausschnitt aus dem Barbereich («Jazz») innerhalb des Restaurationsbereichs

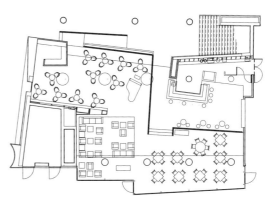

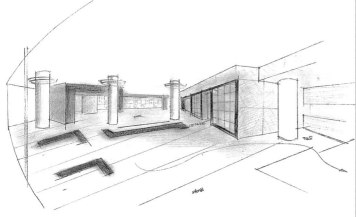

Example of another structural sketches for the restaurant area

Beispiel für weitere strukturelle Skizzen zu dem Restaurant-Bereich

Plan of the Tizian Restaurant area   Tizian Restaurant area (light fixtures after Tizian; Claudia Meythaler)

Grundriß «Tizian»   Restaurationsbereich «Tizian» (Leuchtkasten nach Tizian; Claudia Meythaler)

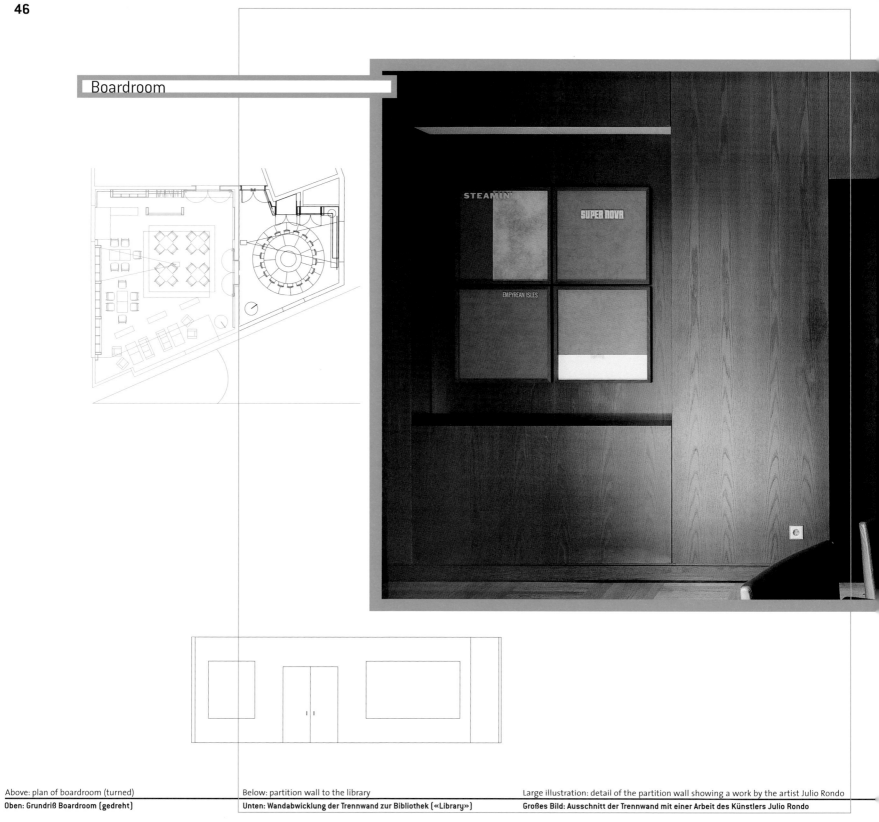

Boardroom

Above: plan of boardroom (turned)

Oben: Grundriß Boardroom (gedreht)

Below: partition wall to the library

Unten: Wandabwicklung der Trennwand zur Bibliothek («Library»)

Large illustration: detail of the partition wall showing a work by the artist Julio Rondo

Großes Bild: Ausschnitt der Trennwand mit einer Arbeit des Künstlers Julio Rondo

Detail of the partition wall with a work by the artist Corsin Fontana

Ausschnitt der Trennwand mit einer Arbeit des Künstlers Corsin Fontana

Library

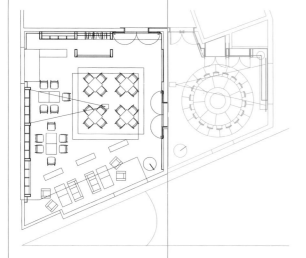

Plan: boardroom / library

Below: library wall

Above: detail of the library

Grundriß: «Boardroom / Library»

Unten: Wandabwicklung der Bibliothek

Oben: Ausschnitt aus der Bibliothek

View from the library (painting: Kurt Hofmann) of the partition wall (oak) between boardroom and library

Blick auf die Trennwand (Eiche) zwischen «Boardroom/Library» aus der Bibliothek (Malerei: Kurt Hofmann)

Standard Room

Plan of the standard rooms (variations with single or double beds)   Illustration: perspective drawing of the standard rooms designed by Hannes Wettstein's office   Left: photographs from the Bauhaus Archives, Berlin

Grundrisse der Standardzimmer (Varianten mit Einzelbett oder Doppelbetten)   Illustration: Perspektivische Vorstellung der Standardzimmer aus dem Büro von Hannes Wettstein   Links: Photographien aus dem Bauhaus-Archiv Berlin

Centre: view from the bed into the bathroom with separate shower / bathtub unit

Above: impression of room (armchair: Capri chair, Hannes Wettstein)

Below: view across the bed of the bath and entrance (right: console with TV)

Mitte: Blick vom Bett in das Bad mit separater Naßzelle (Dusche / Bad)

Oben: Raumeindruck (Sessel «Capri-Chair»; Design: Hannes Wettstein)

Unten: Blick über das Bett auf Bad und Entrée (rechts: Konsole mit TV-Gerät)

Mini Suite

Mini-Suiten (III. bis VI. Etage; 4x)
Größerer Wohnbereich (als Standardzimmer)

Mini suites (3rd to 6th floor, 4x)
With larger living area (as standard room)

Plan of the mini suite
Grundriß «Mini-Suite»

View of the TV console, designed to create a partition
Blick auf das Trennelement mit TV

View of the bed over the partition

Detail with reflection

Blick über das Trennelement auf das Bett

Ausschnitt mit Spiegelung

Corner Suite

Corner-Suiten (II. bis VI. Etage; insgesamt 5x)
Entrée, Gäste-WC, Wohn- und Eßbereich,
Schlafzimmer, großes Bad

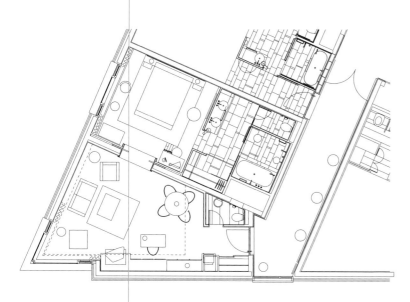

Corner suites (2nd to 6th floor, 5x)
Entrance, guest toilet, living and dining area,
bedroom and large bathroom

View of the bedroom from the living-room (poster by Sigmar Polke)   Detail of the bathroom

Blick vom Wohnraum in das Schlafzimmer (Plakat: Sigmar Polke)   **Ausschnitt aus dem Badezimmer**

Executive Suite

Executive-Suiten (II. und IV. bis VI. Etage; insgesamt 4x)
Flur, Gäste-WC, Wohn und Eßbereich, großes Badezimmer,
Schlafzimmer und begehbarer Kleiderschrank

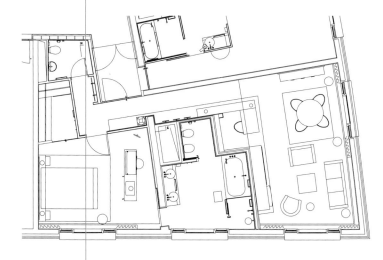

Executive suites (2nd and 4th to 6th floor, 4x)
Hall, guest toilet, living and dining area, large bathroom,
bedroom and walk-in wardrobe

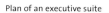
Plan of an executive suite | Illustration: perspective drawing of the projected layout by Hannes Wettstein's office | Detail of an integrated workplace (corner element by Hannes Wettstein)

Grundriß einer «Executive»-Suite | **Illustration: Perspektivische Vorstellung der späteren Raumsituation aus dem Büro von Hannes Wettstein** | **Ausschnitt des integrierten Arbeitsplatzes («Eckelement» von Hannes Wettstein)**

Detail of a dressing table in the bedroom, with reflection

Detail des Schminktisches im Schlafzimmer mit Spiegelung

Presidential Suite (Daimler)

Gesamtfläche ca.   165,0 m²
davon Wohnen / Essen ca.   72,0 m²
(inkl. Kaminecke)
zusätzlich: Flur, Gäste-WC, Küche, großes Badezimmer,
Schlafzimmer und begehbarer Kleiderschrank

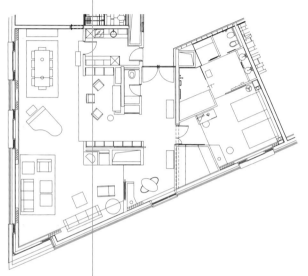

Total area approx.   165 m²
Living and dining area approx.   72 m²
(incl. fireside corner)
Hall, guest toilet, living and dining area, large bathroom,
bedroom and walk-in wardrobe

Plan of the presidential suite (Daimler)   Illustration: perspective drawing of the projected layout by Hannes Wettstein's office   View of the dining table from the TV-corner

Grundriß der Presidential Suite (Daimler)   **Illustration: Perspektivische Vorstellung der späteren Raumsituation aus dem Büro von Hannes Wettstein**   **Blick aus der TV-Ecke auf den Eßtisch**

View of the open fire from the three-piece suite
Blick von der Sofagruppe auf die Kaminecke

Presidential Suite (Maybach)

Gesamtfläche ca.	176,0 m²
davon Wohnen/Essen ca.	72,0 m²
separates Konferenzzimmer ca.	28,0 m²

zusätzlich: Flur, Küche, großes Badezimmer, Gäste-WC,
Schlafzimmer und begehbarer Kleiderschrank

Total area approx.	176 m²
Living and dining area approx.	72 m²
Separate conference room, approx.	28 m²

Hall, kitchen, large bathroom, guest toilet,
bedroom and walk-in wardrobe

Plan of the presidential suite (Maybach) Above: three piece suite with a view of Marlene-Dietrich-Platz Below left: detail of the storage space/rack in the hallway Below right: reading corner in the bedroom

Grundriß der Presidential Suite (Maybach) **Oben: Sofagruppe mit Ausblick auf den Marlene-Dietrich-Platz** **Unten links: Detail der Ablage im Flur** **Unten rechts: Leseecke im Schlafzimmer**

View of the conference room from the three piece suite and across the dining table; to the left: the integrated partition wall (with TV) to the dining area and hallway

Blick von der Sofagruppe über den Eßtisch in das Konferenzzimmer; im Anschnitt links die integrierte Trennwand (mit TV) zum Eßbereich und Flur

Regency Club

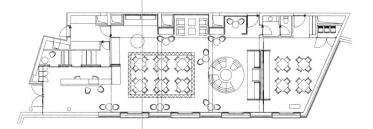

Plan of the Regency Club on the 7th floor

Grundriß des «Regency»-Clubs in der VII. Etage

Detail of one of the niches (photographs of the International Film Festival Berlin)

Detail aus einer der Nischen (Photographien von den Int. Filmfestspielen Berlin)

Detail of the room

Ausschnitt aus der Raumsituation

The separate area with wall design by the Geneva artist Sylvie Fleury

Der separate Bereich mit Wandarbeit der Genfer Künstlerin Sylvie Fleury

John Armleder, Monika Baer, Sylvie Fleury, Günther Förg, Corsin Fontana,
Eberhard Havekost,
Ingrid Hartlieb,
Kurt Hofmann,
Hubert Kiecol,
Karin Kneffel,
Imi Knoebel,
Rupprecht Matthies,
Gerold Miller,
Nader,
Susanne Paesler,
Gert Rappenecker,
Julio Rondo,
Jo Schöpfer,
Dirk Skreber,
Sybille Ungers,
Peter Zimmermann,
Otto Zitko

ART

Dorothea Strauss

In einer langen Nacht im Grand Hyatt Berlin

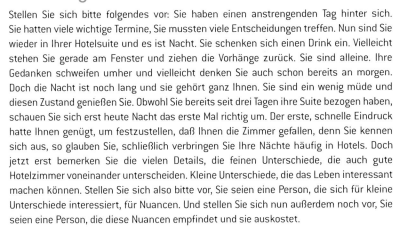

Stellen Sie sich bitte folgendes vor: Sie haben einen anstrengenden Tag hinter sich. Sie hatten viele wichtige Termine, Sie mussten viele Entscheidungen treffen. Nun sind Sie wieder in Ihrer Hotelsuite und es ist Nacht. Sie schenken sich einen Drink ein. Vielleicht stehen Sie gerade am Fenster und ziehen die Vorhänge zurück. Sie sind alleine. Ihre Gedanken schweifen umher und vielleicht denken Sie auch schon bereits an morgen. Doch die Nacht ist noch lang und sie gehört ganz Ihnen. Sie sind ein wenig müde und diesen Zustand genießen Sie. Obwohl Sie bereits seit drei Tagen ihre Suite bezogen haben, schauen Sie sich erst heute Nacht das erste Mal richtig um. Der erste, schnelle Eindruck hatte Ihnen genügt, um festzustellen, daß Ihnen die Zimmer gefallen, denn Sie kennen sich aus, so glauben Sie, schließlich verbringen Sie Ihre Nächte häufig in Hotels. Doch jetzt erst bemerken Sie die vielen Details, die feinen Unterschiede, die auch gute Hotelzimmer voneinander unterscheiden. Kleine Unterschiede, die das Leben interessant machen können. Stellen Sie sich also bitte vor, Sie seien eine Person, die sich für kleine Unterschiede interessiert, für Nuancen. Und stellen Sie sich nun außerdem noch vor, Sie seien eine Person, die diese Nuancen empfindet und sie auskostet.

Sind Sie ein neugieriger Mensch, der sich überraschen lassen kann? Sie behaupten es zumindest von sich. Sie leben Ihr Leben nach bestimmten Maximen und wissen, daß Sie es im Moment recht sorgenfrei leben können. Aber denken Sie auch noch daran, daß sich das Leben in unerwarteter Weise plötzlich sehr schnell verändern kann? In einer Weise, die Sie heute vielleicht überhaupt nicht in Betracht ziehen? So etwas kann geschehen. Stellen Sie sich also weiter vor, Sie liebten Gedankenspiele, Sie liebten es sich zu fragen, was wäre wenn? Wenn Sie aber am Tag träumen, tun Sie das dann mit doppeltem Netz? Oder leben Sie auch Ihre Träume? Glauben Sie an Ihre Träume? Also gut, dann stellen Sie sich nun bitte auch noch vor, Sie liebten es zu träumen, und dies obwohl Sie auch in der Lage sind, pragmatisch zu handeln, oder gerade deshalb, denn schließlich könnten Sie sich auch eine Suite in diesem Hotel leisten.

So, und nun gehört die Nacht ganz Ihnen, Ihnen und was Sie daraus machen.

Als Kind habe ich die große Eingangstür des Hauses, in dem unsere Familie gewohnt hat, immer mit großem Schwung aufgestoßen, denn bevor sie wieder ins Schloß fiel, musste ich es bis zum vierten Stock geschafft haben. Parallel dazu sagte ich laut die Reihe der Primzahlen auf, die jeweils ganz verschiedenen Türen bis nach oben zugeordnet >s.95

0 cm   40 cm

0 cm

30 cm

Monika Baer

MONIKA BAER wurde 1964 in Freiburg im Breisgau geboren;
lebt und arbeitet in Düsseldorf.

Born 1964 in Freiburg; lives and works in Düsseldorf.

Einzelausstellungen / Solo Shows

1998   Portikus Frankfurt (mit Paul McCarthy) (K)
       Bonner Kunstverein (mit J. Wohnseifer) (K)
       Luis Campaña, Köln

1997   Le Case d'Arte, Milano
       Kunsthalle St. Gallen (K)

1995/1996   Luis Campaña, Köln

1993   Luis Campaña, Köln

(K) = Katalog / Catalog

o.T., 1992   o.T., 1992

Untitled, 1992   *Untitled*, 1992

Executive suite (Room No. 220):
View of the dining area and the pantry

**Executive-Suite (Zimmer-Nr. 220):
Blick auf Eßecke und Anrichte**

Cuddly Painting, (2 Bilder aus der Serie «Cuddly Painting», 1996; Kunstfell, violett, 30 x 30 cm, je eines in den Corner Suiten 342 und 542)

Cuddly Painting, (2 paintings from the *Cuddly Painting* series, 1996, imitation fur, violet, 30 x 30 cm, one in each of the junior suites 352 and 542)

Sylvie Fleury

0 cm   30 cm

0 cm

30 cm

Andere Arbeiten / Other works:
Regency-Club, Wallpainting:
«Be Amazing», 1998

SYLVIE FLEURY wurde 1961 in Genf geboren; lebt und arbeitet in Genf.

Born 1961 in Geneva; lives and works in Geneva.

Einzelausstellungen seit / Solo Shows since 1991

1999/2000 Elizabeth Cherry Contemporary Art, Tucson

1998 "All You need", Gallery Side 2, Tokyo
"Life can get heavy, Mascara shouldn't", Galerie Laure Genillard, London
Galerie Philomene Magers, München
Galerie Art & Public, Genève
Galerie Mehdi Chouakri, Berlin
ACE Gallery, Los Angeles
Migros Museum, Museum für Gegenwartskunst, Zürich (K)
Villa Merkel, Galerie der Stadt Esslingen

1997 Galeria Modulo, Lisboa
"Spring", Galerie Philomene Magers, Köln
"Envy", Rebecca Camhi Gallery, Athens
"Skin Crimes", Galerie Bob van Orsouw, Zürich
"Bedroom Ensemble", Galerie Mehdi Chouakri, Berlin
"Is Your Makeup Crashproof?", Postmasters Gallery, New York
"Ultravivid", Elizabeth Cherry Contemporary Art, Tucson

1996 Galleria Il Capricorno, Venezia
"First Spaceship on Venus", MAMCO, Genève
Le Case d'Arte, Milano

1993 Postmasters Gallery, New York
Hervé Mikaeloff c/o Emanuel Perrotin, Paris
Galerie 121, Antwerpen
Galerie Bob van Orsouw, Zürich
"The Art of Survival", Neue Galerie am Landesmuseum
Joanneum, Graz (K)
Galerie Gilbert Brownstone, Paris
Galerie Paludetto, Torino
"The Art of Survival / Baby Doll Lounge", with Angela Bulloch,
Lore Genillard Gallery, London

1992 Centre d'Art Contemporain, Martigny
Galerie van Gelder, Amsterdam
Postmasters Gallery, New York
Galerie Porte-Avion, Marseille

1991 Galerie Art & Public, Genève
Galerie Rivolta, Lausanne
"Vital Perfection", Galerie Philomene Magers, Bonn (K)

Galerie Christine König, Wien
"Moisturizing is the answer", Galerie Mehdi Chouakri, Berlin
ECAL, Lausanne

1995 Galerie Susanna Kulli, St. Gallen
Galerie Art & Public, Genève
Galeria The Box, Torino
Galerie der Stadt Esslingen
Galerie TRE, Stockholm
Museum of Contemporary Art, Chicago
Galerie Gilbert Brownstone, Paris
Postmasters Gallery, New York

1994 "Escape", Le Consortium, Dijon
La Maison des Jeunes, Neuchâtel
Postmasters Gallery, New York
Galerie Philomene Magers, Köln
Gallery Sarah Cottier, Sidney

(K) = Katalog / Catalog

Corner suite:
view into the bedroom from the living-room

Corner-Suite:
Blick vom Wohnraum in das Schlafzimmer

Arbeit aus einer Serie, «o.T.», 1997; Serie von 4 Aquarellen, (je 32 x 41 cm; Inv.-Nr. 1087 - IFB 03504, 03506, 03516, 03496), je gehängt als Zweier-Set in der «Daimler»-Suite im Wohnbereich und Schlafzimmer

Work from a series *Untitled* 1997; series of four watercolours, (32 x 41 cm each; invt.-No. 1087 - IFB 03504, 03506, 03516, 03496), each hanging as a pair in the Daimler suite in the living area and in the bedroom

0 cm   41 cm

Günther Förg

0 cm

32 cm

GÜNTHER FÖRG wurde 1952 in Füssen geboren; lebt in Areuse, Schweiz.

Born 1952 in Füssen; lives in Areuse, Switzerland.

Einzelausstellungen (Auswahl) seit / Solo Shows (selection) since 1985

1999   "Günther Förg", Wanderausstellung, Sammlung Deutsche Bank (K)

1998/1999   "Was andern selbstverständlich ist, ist uns Problem",
Museum Abteiberg, Mönchengladbach (K)

1998   "Günther Förg", Museo Reina Sofia, Madrid (K)
"Aquarelle", Ursula Blickle Stiftung, Kraichtal (K)
Stadtgalerie, Kulturring Sundern

1997   Haus für konstruktive und konkrete Kunst, Zürich (K)

1996   Kunstverein Hamburg
"Gitterbilder", Kunstmuseum Luzern (mit Thomas Hirschhorn) (K)

1995/1996   Kunstverein Hannover

1995   "Günther Förg, Paintings 1974–1994", Stedelijk Museum Amsterdam (K)

1994   "Druckgraphische Serien", Kunstmuseum Bonn (K)
Kunsthalle Winterthur

1993   Camden Art Center, London

1991   Touko Museum of Contemporary Art, Tokyo
Musée d'Art Moderne de la Ville de Paris (K)
"Masken", Kunstverein München (K)
Dallas Museum of Art, Dallas

1990/1991   Museum Fridericianum Kassel / Museum van Hedendaagse Kunst, Gent /
Museum der Bildenden Künste Leipzig / Kunsthalle Tübingen (K) /
Wiener Secession, Wien (K)

1990   "Stations of the Cross",
The Renaissance Society at the University of Chicago (K)
The Chinati Foundation, Marfa

1989   Newport Harbor Art Museum, Newport Beach /
Museum of Modern Art, San Francisco /
Milwaukee Art Museum, Milwaukee (K)
Castello di Rivoli, Torino (K)
"Günther Förg – Gesamte Editionen / The Complete
Editions 1974–1988",
Museum Boymans-van-Beuningen, Rotterdam /
Neue Galerie am Landesmuseum, Graz (K)

1987/1988   Museum Haus Lange, Krefeld / Maison de la Culture,
St. Etienne / Haags Gemeente Museum, Den Haag (K)

1986   Kunsthalle Bern / Westfälischer Kunstverein, Münster (K)

1985   Stedelijk Museum, Amsterdam (mit Jeff Wall)

(K) = Katalog / Catalog

2 Arbeiten aus einer Serie «o.T.», 1997/98; Serie von 8 Aquatinten,
je 60 x 40 cm; Papierformat 80 x 60, je 2 Sets in den Suiten 242, 442, 642

Two works from the series *Untitled*, 1997/98; series of eight aquatints,
60 x 40 cm each; paper format 80 x 60, two sets each in suites 242, 442, 642

Presidential suite (Maybach):
view of the threepiece suite from the workplace

Presidential-Suite (Maybach):
Blick vom Arbeitsplatz auf die Sofagruppe

0 cm   38 cm

0 cm

48 cm

Corsin Fontana

CORSIN FONTANA wurde 1944 in Domat / Ems (Graubünden, Schweiz) geboren; Lehre und Arbeit als Offsetdrucker; seit 1967 freischaffend künstlerisch tätig; lebt und arbeitet seit 1967 in Basel.

Born 1944 in Domat / Ems; lives and works in Basel.

Einzelausstellungen (Auswahl) / Solo Shows (selection)

1999   Galerie Tony Wüthrich, Basel

1998   "Zeichnung", Kunsthaus Kunstverein Baselland, Muttenz

1997   Galerie Tony Wüthrich, Basel

1996   Galerie Tony Wüthrich, Basel

1994   Galerie Kornfeld, Zürich

1993   Kunstverein Dortmund

1991   Kunsthalle Winterthur

1988   Galerie Littmann, Basel (K)

1986   Galerie Emmerich-Baumann, Zürich

1985   "Arbeiten 1980–85", Kunsthaus Zürich (K)

1983   Galerie Claudia Knapp, Chur

1982   "Das Auslöschen der Bilder durch die Zeit", Galerie Gimpel-Hanover & André Emmerich, Zürich
"Das Auslöschen der Bilder durch die Zeit", Galerie Stampa, Basel

Andere Arbeiten / Other works:
Boardroom / Library; 6 Arbeiten aus der Serie «Klänge»; 1998; Wachskreide auf Papier

Boardroom/library; six works from the *Sounds* series, 1998;
Wax crayon on paper

1981   Galerie Buchmann, St. Gallen

1980   Kunsthalle Palazzo, Liestal

1979   Galerie Buchmann, St. Gallen

1977   Galerie Buchmann, St. Gallen

1976   Galerie Stampa, Basel

1973   Galerie Nächst St. Stephan, Wien (K)
Galerie Stampa, Basel (K)

1975   Galerie Space, Wiesbaden
Bündner Kunstmuseum, Chur

1971   "Strassenaktionen", Galerie Stampa, Basel
"Fotoleinwände", Galerie Stampa, Basel

1968   Galerie Impact, Lausanne

(K) = Katalog / Catalog

2 Arbeiten aus der Serie «Klänge»; 1998; (Wachskreide auf Papier)

Two works from the *Sounds* series, 1998 (wax crayon on paper)

Executive suite (Room Nr. 520):
detail of a sofa in the living area

Executive-Suite (Zimmer-Nr. 520):
Ausschnitt des Sofas im Wohnbereich

Eberhard Havekost

EBERHARD HAVEKOST wurde 1967 in Dresden geboren;
1991–96 Studium an der HfbK Dresden; lebt und
arbeitet in Dresden.

Born 1967 in Dresden; lives and works in Dresden.

Einzelausstellungen / Solo Shows

1999   Galerie für Zeitgenössische Kunst, Leipzig
Statements, Art Basel
Kontakt, Galerie Gebr. Lehmann, Dresden

1998/1999   Geiz, Luxus, (mit F. Nitsche),
Kulturwissenschaftliches Institut, Essen

1998   Leinwandhaus, Frankfurt a. M.
Fenster-Fenster, Kunstmuseum Luzern (K)
ZOOM, Anton Kern Gallery, New York

1997   Frieren, Galerie Gebr. Lehmann, Dresden
Förderkoje, ART COLOGNE, Köln

1995   Wärme, Galerie Gebr. Lehmann, Dresden (mit Th. Scheibitz; K)
Galerie Gebr. Lehmann, Dresden

(K) = Katalog / Catalog

Presidential suite (Maybach):
view of the separate conference room

**Presidential-Suite (Maybach):
Blick in das separate Konferenzzimmer**

Hubert Kiecol

HUBERT KIECOL wurde 1950 in Bremen-Blumenthal geboren; 1971 Werkkunstschule Hamburg; 1975 Hochschule für Bildende Künste; seit 1993 Professur an der Kunstakademie Stuttgart; lebt und arbeitet in Köln.

Born 1950 in Bremen-Blumenthal; lives and works in Cologne.

Einzelausstellungen (Auswahl) seit / Solo Shows (selection) since 1981

1999   "Ahab", Hamburger Kunsthalle, Hamburg

1998   Oldenburger Kunstverein, Oldenburg (Leporello)
Staatliche Kunsthalle Karlsruhe (Orangerie), Karlsruhe
Maximilianverlag Sabine Knust, München

1997   "Paradis", FRAC Picardie, Amiens (K)
"Weissaufschwarzdrucke", Galerie Karlheinz Mayer, Karlsruhe
Galerie Bärbel Grässlin, Frankfurt a. M.

1996   Produzentengalerie, Hamburg

1995   Kunstverein Wolfsburg (K)
Galerie Bärbel Grässlin, Frankfurt a. M.

1994   Narodni Galerie v Praze, Ifa-Institut für Auslandsbeziehungen, Prag
Maximilianverlag Sabine Knust, München
Kunstverein Heilbronn
Jablonka Galerie, Köln
Kunststation Sankt Peter, Köln

1993   Galerie Beaumont, Luxembourg
Galerie Karlheinz Mayer, Karlsruhe
Eleni Koroneau Gallery, Athens

1992   Galerie Bärbel Grässlin, Frankfurt a. M.
Bruno Brunnet Fine Arts, Berlin
Galerie Ascan Crone und Produzentengalerie, Hamburg

1991   Galerie Juana de Aizpuru, Madrid
Kunsthalle Nürnberg (K)
Jänner Galerie, Wien
Galerie Gisela Capitain, Köln

1990   Luhring Augustine Gallery, New York
Villa Arson, Nice (Heft)
Galerie Max Hetzler, Köln
Westfälischer Kunstverein, Münster (K)

1989   Galerie Peter Pakesch, Wien
Asher/Faure Gallery, Los Angeles

1988   Städtisches Kunstmuseum, Bonn (K)
Galerie Max Hetzler, Köln
Galerie Gisela Capitain, Köln
Galerie Grässlin-Erhardt, Frankfurt a. M. (Leporello)
Galerie Lia Rumma, Napoli
PPS Galerie, F.C. Gundlach, Hamburg (mit Werner Büttner)

1987   Galerie Ursula Schurr, Stuttgart
Galerie Reinhard Onnasch, Berlin
Galerie Max Hetzler, Köln

1986   Forum Kunst, Rottweil
"Zeichnungen", Galerie Borgmann-Capitain, Köln
Galerie Grässlin-Erhardt, Frankfurt a. M.
"5 Skulpturen", Galerie Max Hetzler, Köln

1985   Galerie Bärbel Grässlin, Frankfurt a. M.
Museum Haus Esters, Krefeld
"Zeichnungen", Galerie Max Hetzler, Köln

1984   Kunstverein Braunschweig (K)
Haus Salve Hospes, Braunschweig
Galerie Max Hetzler, Köln

1983   Produzentengalerie, Hamburg

1982   Galerie Max Hetzler, Stuttgart
Galerie Arno Kohnen, Düsseldorf

1981   Produzentengalerie, Hamburg

(K) = Katalog / Catalog

Serie von 4 Aquatinta-Radierungen «Astronomieblau», 1994; 94 x 64,5
cm (Papierformat 107 x 76 cm), je 2 in einer Corner Suite 342 und 542

Series of four aquatint etchings: *Astronomy Blue*, 1994,
94 x 64.5 cm (paper format 107 x 76 cm), two each in
corner suites 342 and 542

Corner suite (Room No. 342):
view of the threepiece suite in the living area

**Corner-Suite (Zimmer-Nr. 342): Blick auf die
Sofagruppe im Wohnbereich der Suite**

0 cm

0 cm 58 cm

0 cm

Karin Kneffel

78 cm

KARIN KNEFFEL wurde 1957 in Marl geboren; 1977–81 Studium der Germanistik und Philosophie, Westfälische Wilhelmsuniversität Münster und Gesamthochschule Duisburg; 1981–87 Studium an der Staatlichen Kunstakademie Düsseldorf bei Johannes Brus und Norbert Tadeusz; Meisterschülerin bei Gerhard Richter; lebt und arbeitet in Düsseldorf.

Born 1957 in Marl; lives and works in Düsseldorf.

Einzelausstellungen seit / Solo Shows since 1984

1998   Galerie Jousse Séguin, Paris
Galerie Johnen & Schöttle, Köln

1997   Accademia Tedesca, Villa Massimo, Roma (K)
Galerie Rüdiger Schöttle, München
Galerie Bob van Orsouw, Zürich

1996   Le Case d'Arte, Galerie Pasquale Leccese, Milano
Forum Kunst, Rottweil (K)

1995   The Corridor, H. Th. Fridjonsson, Reykjavik
Galerie Schönewald und Beuse, Krefeld

1994   Kunstverein Bremerhaven
Galerie Wanda Reiff, Amsterdam
Kunstverein Heilbronn
Galerie Jousse Séguin, Paris
Kunstverein Lingen (K)
Het Kruithuis, Museum voor Hedendaagse Kunst, s'Hertogenbosch (K)

1989   Galerie Tabea Langenkamp, Düsseldorf
Galerie Sophia Ungers, Köln

1988   Raum 404, Heidelberg

1984   Galerie Rüdiger Schöttle, München (mit Elke Denda)

1993   Galerie Senda, Barcelona
ART COLOGNE, Einzelkoje der Galerie Sophia Ungers, Köln (K)

1992   Galerie Schütz, Frankfurt a. M.
Galerie Rüdiger Schöttle, Paris
Galerie Tabea Langenkamp, Düsseldorf
ART COLOGNE, Förderkoje der Galerie Schütz, Frankfurt a. M.

1991   Galerie Sophia Ungers, Köln
Galerie Rüdiger Schöttle, München

1990   Galerie Schütz, Frankfurt a. M.
Dr. A. H. Murken, Gütersloh

(K) = Katalog / Catalog

«Pfirsiche», 1996; 78 x 58cm, Aquarell auf Büttenpapier

Peach, 1996, 78 x 58 cm, watercolour on handmade paper

Executive suite (Room No. 620):
detail of the sofa in the living area

**Executive-Suite (Zimmer-Nr. 620):
Ausschnitt des Sofas im Wohnbereich**

0 cm   73 cm

0 cm

102,5 cm

Imi Knoebel

IMI KNOEBEL wurde 1940 in Dessau geboren; 1964–1971 Studium an der Staatlichen Kunstakademie Düsseldorf; lebt in Düsseldorf.

Born 1940 in Dessau; lives in Düsseldorf.

Einzelausstellungen seit / Solo Shows since 1993

1999   "Ajun Musa", Galerie Grässlin, Frankfurt a. M.
"Mennige – Serie", ifa-Galerie, Bonn
Galerie Lea Gredt, Luxembourg
Galerie Vera Munro, Hamburg
"New Paintings", Akira Ikeda Gallery, Nagoya (K)

1998   "Rot Gelb Weiß Blau", Galerie am Lindenplatz, Schaan/Liechtenstein
Galerie Fahnemann, Berlin
"IMI für Deutschland", Institut, Düsseldorf
"Fluorescent Works", Art & Public, Genève
"schön wär's", Thaddaeus Ropac, Salzburg (K)

1997   "Imi Knoebel Retrospektive 1968–1996", IVAM Centre del Carme, Valencia (K)
Jablonka Galerie, Köln
Galerie Bärbel Grässlin, Frankfurt a. M.
"Imi Knoebel – Eine Ausstellung", Kunsthalle Düsseldorf (K)
"Tag und Nacht & Bunt", Kunstmuseum Luzern (K)
"Imi Knoebel Œuvres 1968–1996", Musée de Grenoble (K)
Galeria Helga de Alvear, Madrid
"Projektionen 1968–1974", Galerie Walcheturm, Zürich
Galerie Erhard Klein, Bad Münstereifel

1994   Galerie Six Friedrich, München
Achenbach Kunsthandel, Düsseldorf (K)
"Odyshape", Galerie Hans Strelow, Düsseldorf
"Chaos mit Ordnung", Tochigi Prefectural Museum of Fine Art (K)
"Phosphorsandwiches", Museum Friedericianum, Kassel
"Rot Gelb Weiß Blau", Galerie Bärbel Grässlin, Frankfurt a. M.
"Rot Gelb Weiß Blau", Galerie Nächst St. Stephan, Wien
"Rot Gelb Weiß Blau", Städtische Kunstsammlungen, Chemnitz (K)
"8 Bilder", Galerie Fahnemann, Berlin (K)

1993   "Portraits", Kanransha, Tokyo
"Sittin' in the morning sun", Galerie Vera Munro, Hamburg
Galerie Six Friedrich, München
Akira Ikeda Gallery, Taura
"Zeichnungen", Städtische Galerie, Quakenbrück

1996   "Zeichnungen", Galerie Fahnemann, Berlin
"Rot Gelb Weiss Blau", Ludwigforum, Aachen (K)
"Jena Bilder", Kunsthistorisches Seminar, Kustodie und Institut für Philosophie, Jena (K)
"Linienbilder 1966–68", Kunstverein St. Gallen, Kunstmuseum, St. Gallen (K)
"Zeichnungen", Galerie Wilma Loock, St. Gallen
"Rot-Weiss", Deutsche Bank, Luxembourg (K)
"Grace Kelly", Gallery Hyundai, Seoul
"Imi Knoebel", Deutsche Bank Wanderausstellung (K)
Akira Ikeda Gallery, Tokyo
"Imi Knoebel Retrospektive 1968–1996", Haus der Kunst, München (K)
"Imi Knoebel Retrospektive 1968–1996", Stedelijk Museum, Amsterdam (K)

1995   "Rot Gelb Weiß Blau", Galerie Wilma Lock, St. Gallen
"Works on paper", Goethe Institut Gallery, London (K)
"Rot Gelb Weiß Blau", Stadtgalerie Kulturring Sundern
"Rot Gelb Weiß Blau", Galerie Six Friedrich, München
"Rot Gelb Weiß Blau", Moderna Galeria, Ljubljana (K)

(K) = Katalog / Catalog

«Grace Kelly», 5 Farblithographien (Drucker: «Derriere L'Etoile Studios», New York)
je 102,5 x 73 cm (Papierformat), je ein Blatt pro Suite

Grace Kelly, five colour lithographs (printed by Derriere L'Etoile Studios, New York), 102,5 x 73 cm (paper format) each, one print in each suite

81

Mini suite (on four standard floors):
corner seating unit

**Mini-Suite (auf 4 «Standard»-Geschoßen vorhanden):
Die Sitzecke**

0 cm   50 cm

0 cm

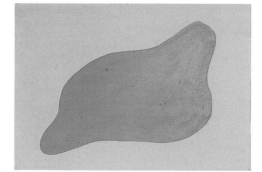

35 cm

Rupprecht Matthies

RUPPRECHT MATTHIES wurde 1959 in Hamburg geboren; 1980–82 Soziologiestudium; 1985 Gründung von «Westwerk» Hamburg; 1989 «Ars Viva» Förderpreis des BDI, Overbekgesellschaft Lübeck; Fridericianum Kassel, Kunstverein Stuttgart (K); 1990 «10. Hamburger Arbeitsstipendium», Kunsthaus, Hamburg (K); 1991 Förderkoje, ART COLOGNE, Köln; 1993 Veranstalter des «dualen Pinsels» für Malerei 2000, Hamburg und Malmö; 1995 Künstlerstätte Bleckede; 1996 «Artists in Residence», Wien; lebt und arbeitet in Hamburg.

Born 1959 in Hamburg; lives and works in Hamburg.

Einzelausstellungen / Solo Shows
1999   Galerie Rüdiger Schöttle, München
         Galerie Paul, Bremerhaven
         Werkstatt Schloss, Wolfsburg

1998   Raum für aktuelle Kunst, Martin Janda, Wien
         Kunstverein, Ludwigsburg

1997   Produzentengalerie, Hamburg
         Galerie Almut Gerber, Köln

1996   Stefan Kalmar, London

1994   "The Best of the Blup", Künstlerhaus Hamburg

1991   "Drei Versuche über keine Ahnung", Produzentengalerie, Hamburg (K)
         "Recht Matt", Kunstraum Neue Kunst, Hannover

1989   Produzentengalerie, Hamburg (K)

1988   Westwerk, Hamburg

1987   Ausstellungsraum Fettstraße, Hamburg

1986   Westwerk, Hamburg

(K) = Katalog / Catalog

2 der 3 Arbeiten aus der Serie «The Best of the Blup»:
115 x 28 cm (grün / weiss), 40 x 20 cm (blau / rosa)

Two of the three works from the series: *The Best of the Blup,*
115 x 28 cm (*Green / White*), 40 x 20 cm (*Blue / Pink*)

Executive suite (Room No. 620):
view of the dining area with sideboard

Executive-Suite (Zimmer-Nr. 620):
Blick auf Essecke mit Anrichte

0 cm   150 cm

0 cm

120 cm

Nader

NADER wurde 1964 in Shiraz (Iran) geboren; Kunstakademie, Stuttgart; PS1 Stipendium, New York; lebt und arbeitet in Berlin.

Born 1964 in Shiraz; lives and works in Berlin.

Einzelausstellungen / Solo Shows

1999   "Equilibrium, intensity and mental geometry of the philosopher S.", Klosterfelde, Hamburg

1998   "The Quantitative Ontology of Reality", The Project, New York
"Revolution der Viadukte", Klosterfelde, Berlin

1997   Helga Maria Klosterfelde, Hamburg
"Ein moralisch-metaphysisches Moment", Kunsthalle St. Gallen (K)
c/o: Atle Gerhardsen, Oslo

1996   "Aristoteles auf dem Eismeer", Klosterfelde, Berlin
Lukas & Hoffmann, Köln

1995   Wiensowski & Harbord, Berlin

1993   Kunstinstitut, Stuttgart

Andere Arbeiten / Other works:
- **Corner-Suiten 242 / 442 / 642;** (je 2 Arbeiten inkl. der oben abgebildeten)
- **Executive-Suite 420**

- **Corner suites 242 / 442 / 642;** (two works in each suite, incl. those shown above)
- **Executive suite 420**

(K) = Katalog / Catalog

Four pages from the series *The Dog Doesn't Lie* (1996);
Indian ink and ink on paper DIN A4

Presidential suite (Maybach):
Detail of the bedroom

**Presidential-Suite (Maybach):
Ausschnitt aus dem Schlafzimmer**

Susanne Paesler

SUSANNE PAESLER wurde 1963 in Darmstadt geboren; 1986–92 Studium an der HdK
Frankfurt a. M., «Städelschule» bei Thomas Bayrle, Jörg Immendorff und Isa Genzken;
1993 Preis «Junger Westen», Kunsthalle Recklinghausen; 1994 «Internationales
Atelier-programm», Künstlerhaus Bethanien, Berlin; 1995 Preis der «Jürgen Ponto
Stiftung», Frankfurt a. M.; Arbeitsstipendium Kunstfonds Bonn; lebt und arbeitet in Berlin.

Born 1963 in Darmstadt; lives and works in Berlin.

Einzelausstellungen / Solo Shows

1997   Zwinger Galerie, Berlin

1996   Zwinger Galerie, Berlin

1995   Künstlerhaus Bethanien, Berlin

o.T., zweiteilig, 1992; Lack auf Aluminium, je 32 x 37,5 cm

Untitled, in two parts, 1992, varnish on aluminium,
32 x 37.5 cm each

Presidential suite (Daimler): view of the sideboard behind the
dining table; to the right: entrance to an additional standard room

**Presidential-Suite (Daimler): Blick auf die Anrichte hinter dem
Eßtisch; Durchgang zu einem zusätzlichen Standardzimmer**

o.T. # 41 aus der Werkgruppe der «Sublime Paintings», 1998;
Autolack auf Öl auf Leinwand

Untitled, # 41 from the group of works: *Sublime Paintings*, 1998,
car paint on oil on canvas

0 cm

130 cm

0 cm

175 cm

Gert Rappenecker

GERT RAPPENECKER wurde 1955 in Freiburg im Breisgau geboren; 1976–1980 Studium an der Accademia di Belle Arti, Florenz / Carrara; 1980–1984 Studium an der Akademie der Bildenden Künste, Stuttgart; lebt und arbeitet in Frankfurt a. M.

Born 1955 in Freiburg im Breisgau; lives and works in Frankfurt a. M.

Einzelausstellungen / Solo Shows

1999/2000 Galerie Martina Detterer, Frankfurt a. M.

1999 Kunsthalle St. Gallen

1998 Galerie Menotti, Baden bei Wien (mit Constanze Ruhm)

1997 Galerie Martina Detterer, Frankfurt a. M.
Galerie Renos Xippas, Paris

1996 Megan Fox Gallery, Santa Fe

1995 Galerie Martina Detterer, Frankfurt a. M. (K)

1994 Galerie Philippe Rizzo, Paris
"Résidence Secondaire", Paris (K)

1993 Galerie Martina Detterer, Frankfurt a. M. (K)

1991 Galerie Martina Detterer, Frankfurt a. M.
Galerie Karin Schorm, Wien

1987 Kunststiftung Baden-Württemberg, Stuttgart (K)

1986 Galerie Achim Kubinski, Stuttgart
Galerie Isabella Kacprzak, Stuttgart

Andere Arbeiten / Other works:
- **Location: Spa** «o. T. » («Triptychon»; 1990/91); Aluminiumguß, Autolack, je 96 x 74 cm

Untitled (triptychs group; 1990/91); Cast aluminium, car paint, 96 x 74 cm each

(K) = Katalog / Catalog

o.T., aus der Werkgruppe der «Landschaften»; Seestück,
1998; Öl auf Fotokopie auf Leinwand, 110 x 150 cm

Untitled, from the group *Landscapes*,
Seascape, 1998, oil on photocopy on
canvas, 110 x 150 cm

Presidential suite (Daimler):
Section of a corner seating unit

Presidential-Suite (Daimler):
Ausschnitt von einer der Sitzecken

«Schablone I», 1998; Öl auf Leinwand   *Pattern I*, 1998, oil on canvas

0 cm

|0 cm |70 cm

Sybille Ungers

SYBILLE UNGERS wurde 1960 in Köln geboren; lebt in Dublin und Köln.

Born 1960 in Cologne; lives in Dublin and Cologne.

Einzelausstellungen (Auswahl) / Solo Shows (selection)

1996   Kerlin Gallery, Dublin

1994   Kerlin Gallery, Dublin

1991   Galerie Max Hetzler, Köln
        Kerlin Gallery, Dublin (K)
        Galerie Gisela Capitain, Köln (K)
        Ric Urmel Gallery, Gent

1990   Galerie Schurr, Stuttgart

1989   Kerlin Gallery, Dublin (K)
        Galerie Paul Andriesse, Amsterdam
        Kunsthalle Düsseldorf (K)
        Art Cologne, Galerie Max Hetzler, Köln

1988   Galerie Schurr, Stuttgart (K)
        Galerie Gisela Capitain, Köln
        Galerie '86, Trier

1987   Galerie Annette Gmeiner Kirchzarten
        Galerie MaxHetzler, Köln

1986   Galerie Schurr, Stuttgart

1985   Ausstellungsraum Fettstraße, Hamburg

90 cm

(K) = Katalog / Catalog

Untitled, 1991; oil on canvas, 70 x 50 cm

Presidential suite (Daimler): view into the walk-in wardrobe;
in the foreground: built-in TV furniture in bedroom

**Presidential-Suite (Daimler): Blick in den Ankleideraum; im
Bildvordergrund eingebautes TV-Möbel im Schlafzimmer**

«Jackson Pollock rot», 1998; Epoxydharz auf Leinwand in Executive-Suite (Zimmer-Nr. 520)

Jackson Pollock Red, 1998; epoxy resin on canvas in the executive suite (Room No. 520)

Peter Zimmermann

0 cm   120 cm

0 cm

140 cm

PETER ZIMMERMANN wurde 1956 in Freiburg im Breisgau geboren; 1978–1983 Studium an der Staatlichen Kunstakademie in Stuttgart; lebt und arbeitet in Köln.

Born 1956 in Freiburg im Breisgau; lives and works in Cologne.

Einzelausstellungen (Auswahl) seit / Solo Shows (selection) since 1988

1999   Galerie Urs Meile, Luzern
Gasser + Grunert Gallery, New York

1998   "Eigentlich könnte alles auch anders sein", Kölnischer Kunstverein, Köln

1997   Otto Dix Haus, Gera
Galerie Kienzle Gmeiner, Berlin
"Boxes and Surfaces", The Agency, London

1996   "Remix", Icebox, Athen
"Öffentlich/Privat", Kunstraum der Universität Lüneburg
Künstlerhaus Stuttgart (mit Thomas Locher)
Galerie Urs Meile, Luzern

1995   Galerie Six Friedrich, München
"Remixes", The Agency, London
"Artist in Residence", Neue Galerie am Landesmuseum Joanneum, Graz (K)
Bacceca Klemens Gasser, Bozen

1994   Galerie Annette Gmeiner, Stuttgart
Galerie Urs Meile, Luzern

1988   Galerie Foncke, Gent

1993   Galerie Tanja Grunert, u. Galerie Zwirner, Köln

1987   Galerie Tanja Grunert, Köln

1992   Kunstverein Münster (K)
Kunstforum München
Kunstverein Ludwigsburg
Galerie HAM, Nagoya

1986   Galerie Annette Gmeiner, Kirchzarten

1991   Galerie Tanja Grunert, Köln

1983   Galerie Tanja Grunert, Stuttgart

1990   Galerie Christian Gögger, München

1989   Galerie Annette Gmeiner, Stuttgart
Galerie Tanja Grunert, Köln (K)
Antiquariat Wögenstein, Wien

(K) = Katalog / Catalog

«Jackson Pollock 20th Century», 1998;
Epoxydharz auf Leinwand, 135 x 110 cm

Jackson Pollock 20th Century, 1998;
epoxy resin on canvas, 135 x 110 cm

Executive suite (Room Nr. 420):
in the foreground: sideboard and integrated workplace

Executive-Suite (Zimmer-Nr. 420):
Im Vordergrund Anrichte und integrierter Arbeitsplatz

A Long Night at the Grand Hyatt Berlin

Dorothea Strauss

Imagine the following situation: you have had an exhausting day. You have had a lot of important appointments, and had to make a number of decisions. You are now back in your hotel suite. It is dark outside. You pour yourself a drink. Perhaps you are standing at the window, and pull back the curtains. You are alone. Your thoughts wander, and maybe you have already started to think about tomorrow. But the night is long, and it belongs to you. You are a little tired – and like the feeling. And although you moved into your suite three days ago, tonight you take a good look around for the first time. The first brief impression was enough to tell you that you liked the rooms; after all, you reckon you know your way around, because you often spend the night at a hotel. But now you begin to notice all the details for the first time, those fine differences that also distinguish good hotel rooms from one another. Barely noticeable differences that can make life interesting. Now, imagine that you are a person who is interested in the little differences, in nuances. And imagine, too, that you are one of t   people who has an eye for these nuances and enjoys them to the full.

Are you the curious type, someone who can take surprises? You certainly claim to be. You live life according to certain maxims and know that you can live quite a carefree life at the moment. But don't forget that your life can suddenly change unexpectedly. In a way that you may not have even considered yet. These things can happen. So imagine that you used to love playing mental games, you used to love asking yourself what would happen if? When you daydream, do you make sure you play safe? Or do you live out your dreams too? Do you believe in your dreams? Well, then just imagine that you used to love your dreams, you loved them although you are also in a position to act pragmatically, or maybe for that very reason, for ultimately you were able to afford a suite in this hotel.

Well, now the night belongs to you, it is yours and all that you make of it.

When I was a child, I always used to give the big entrance door to the house where our family lived an almighty push so that it opened with great momentum, because I had to make it to the fourth floor before it clicked shut. While I was heading up the stairs, I would also say out loud the series of prime numbers assigned to all the very different doors right up to the top, numbers that were also linked to a particular sequence of steps. Sometimes another door would open somewhere or other and complicate matters. But whenever I succeeded I was rewarded: I didn't have to do my homework. – I look out of the window and think about all this. Unfortunately, the house no longer exists. I'd love to see whether I would still manage it today.

People walk past on the street. The windows are closed. I can't hear a sound. After such an exhausting day it is nice to be able to stand around at night in a hotel room, feeling slightly bored and letting time go by. Everything becomes a little unreal, lighter and fuzzy.

I look around my room and catch sight of a picture on the wall. It is a striking picture. Strange I haven't noticed it before. I go and stand at the window again, and then return to the picture. Pictures have always had this incredible hold on me. Does a picture have the power to change your life?

On a recent flight to Chicago, I found myself sitting next to an art collector, a disciplined businesswoman. She was very American, charming, distanced and professional. However, when she spoke about her collection, she lent forward so that her upper body was bent slightly over me, and held my arm rather tightly: "I find it exciting knowing that these pictures belong to me. They are my insurance, my life insurance, because there are lots of things in life I haven't even begun to think about yet. You know, getting involved in art is a way of appropriating the world. Art is a way of appropriating the world."

Art is a way of appropriating the world… These words go through my mind again tonight, words that I laughed about when I heard them, because they seemed to have a touch of pathos. But how do you go about appropriating the world?

It isn't always easy for us to understand what we find really important. In the course of our lives, we play so many different parts on so many different stages. And with such apparent ease.

How do you appropriate the world?

At some time or other, I suddenly noticed that I had lost all contact with art. Something I can't really pin down had gradually disappeared, or maybe I'd never really had it. >p.96

waren und mit einer bestimmten Schrittfolge gekoppelt wurden. Manchmal ging dann noch irgendwo eine weitere Türe auf, das komplizierte die ganze Sache. Doch immer wenn mir dies gelang, entfielen als Lohn die Schulaufgaben. – Ich schaue aus dem Fenster und denke daran. Das Haus gibt es leider nicht mehr. Ich würde sehr gerne versuchen, ob ich es heute noch schaffe.

Auf der Straße laufen Leute vorbei, die Fenster sind geschlossen, ich höre keine Geräusche. Es ist schön, sich nach einem anstrengenden Tag nachts in einem Hotelzimmer ein bißchen zu langweilen, herumzustehen und die Zeit vergehen zu lassen. Alles wird ein wenig unwirklich, es wird leicht und benommen.

Ich schaue mich in meinen Zimmern um und sehe an der Wand ein Bild. Es ist ein auffälliges Bild. Merkwürdig, daß ich es jetzt erst bemerke. Ich stehe wieder am Fenster, und dann wieder vor dem Bild. Bilder haben immer eine große Faszination auf mich ausgeübt.

Ob ein Bild die Kraft besitzt, Ihr Leben zu verändern?

Als ich kürzlich nach Chicago flog, saß ich neben einer Kunstsammlerin, einer disziplinierten Geschäftsfrau; sehr amerikanisch, liebenswürdig, distanziert, professionell. Doch als sie über ihre Sammlung sprach, beugte sie sich mit dem Oberkörper leicht zu mir herüber und hielt etwas zu fest meinen Arm: «Zu wissen, dass diese Bilder mir gehören, erregt mich. Sie sind meine Versicherung; meine Lebensversicherung, da es in diesem Leben noch vieles gibt, an das ich heute nicht mal denke. Wissen Sie, sich mit Kunst zu beschäftigen ist eine Form von Weltaneignung. Kunst ist eine Form von Weltaneignung.»

Kunst ist eine Form von Weltaneignung.... heute Nacht fallen mir diese Worte wieder ein, über die ich damals lachen musste, denn sie erschienen mir doch ein wenig pathetisch. Nur: Wie geht das, Weltaneignung?

Es fällt nicht immer leicht zu verstehen, was für einen wirklich wichtig ist. Man bewegt sich auf so vielen verschiedenen Bühnen. Und das alles scheinbar mühelos.

Wie eignen Sie sich die Welt an?

Irgendwann stellte ich plötzlich fest, daß ich den Anschluss an die Kunst verloren hatte. Etwas, das ich nicht richtig benennen kann, war schleichend verschwunden, oder vielleicht habe ich es auch nie wirklich gehabt. Ich fing an, in zeitgenössische Ausstellungen zu gehen. Kaufte mir Bücher, las in Kunstmagazinen und tastete mich vor, versuchte zu begreifen. Ich fing wieder an, ins Kino zu gehen, wann immer es mir die Zeit erlaubte und ich fing auch wieder an, mir Zeit dafür zu reservieren. Ich verabredete mich mit mir selbst in Ausstellungen, im Theater und schenkte mir Kinobons. Je sicherer ich wurde, über die

verschiedenen Schwellen zu gehen, umso mehr kam ich zu dem Schluß, daß aktuelle Kunst – vielleicht wie noch nie zuvor in der Geschichte – vieles mit mir gemeinsam hat, mit mir als Mensch in einer medialisierten Welt. Aber mit vielen Sehnsüchten. Ich möchte jetzt nicht behaupten, ich sei eine Künstlerin, aber die verschiedenen Versatzstücke, denen ich in Ausstellungen begegnete, erschienen mir plötzlich wie Spiegel meines eigenen Lebens. Ich konnte mich erkennen und mit vielem hatte ich zu tun und mit einigem auch nicht, aber auch darin konnte ich etwas erkennen. Es geht um Entscheidungen. Um Denkmodelle. Und um Möglichkeiten, so glaube ich zumindest. Darin liegt so etwas wie Freiheit.

Die Stunden vergehen. Ich schaue mein Bild an. Es ist ein Original. Ich schaue es genau an und wenn ich die Augen schließe, kann ich es mir bereits vorstellen. Es heißt, der normale Museumsbesucher würde im Durchschnitt nur circa anderthalb Minuten vor einem Kunstwerk stehen bleiben. Das sind 90 Sekunden. Manchmal können 90 Sekunden aber eine kleine Ewigkeit bedeuten, oder?

In der Episode «Crows» aus Akira Kurosawas Film «Dreams» steht ein japanischer Kunststudent (als Kurosawas Alter Ego) in einem Museum vor dem Gemälde van Goghs «Die Brücke von Langlois in Arles». In der nächsten Einstellung läuft dieser junge Mann in genau der Landschaft umher, die er zuvor so intensiv betrachtet hat. Dort begegnet er van Gogh (gespielt von Martin Scorsese) an der Staffelei, der jedoch bald zwischen den Weizenfeldern entschwindet. Der Student begibt sich auf die Suche nach ihm und gerät dabei in die Bilderwelt van Goghs. Aufgrund einer bemerkenswerten Trick-Technik sieht der Zuschauer den jungen Mann durch die gemalten Motive herumlaufen, hinter Häusern verschwinden, die Straße überqueren.

Während ich wieder vor meinem Bild stehe, taucht eine längst vergessene Erinnerung auf, als ich nämlich als Kind zusammen mit meiner Mutter das erste Mal in einem Museum war. Psst, sei ganz, ganz leise, hatte meine Mutter geflüstert. Doch vor einem Gemälde von Hieronymus Bosch fürchtete ich mich so sehr, daß ich zu weinen anfing. Aber das ist doch nur ein Bild, sagte meine Mutter. Wirklich?

Stellen Sie sich bitte folgendes vor: Es ist spät geworden. Sie stehen wieder am Fenster. Wenn Sie jetzt jemand fragen würde, worum es denn eigentlich in Ihrem Bild ginge und was Sie sosehr daran fasziniert, könnten Sie eine Geschichte erzählen, eine, die einiges, aber doch nicht alles erklärt. Und genau das würde Ihnen gefallen. Und vielleicht würden Sie den Nachtportier anrufen und fragen, von wem denn das Bild in Ihrem Zimmer sei? Und Sie würden insistieren, es heute Nacht noch zu erfahren, denn morgen, das würden Sie wissen, morgen ist vielleicht ein anderer Tag. Nun, schlafen Sie gut und träumen Sie davon. Wovon? Was immer Sie sich wünschen. Gute Nacht.

96

«Spindeln», Ingrid Hartlieb; in der
Aufzugslobby in der II. Etage

Spindels, by Ingrid Hartlieb; in the lift lobby of the 2ⁿᵈ floor.

I started going to exhibitions on contemporary art. I bought books, read art magazines, felt my way forwards, trying to understand. I started going to the cinema again whenever time permitted, and I also started to find time to go. I made appointments with myself to go to exhibitions, to the theatre and gave myself presents of cinema vouchers. The more self-assured I became about crossing all these different thresholds, the more I came to the conclusion that the art of today – perhaps more than at any other time in history – had a lot in common with me, with me as a human being in a world dominated by media. But with many different desires. I don't want to claim, at this point, that I am an artist, but all the different set pieces I encountered in exhibitions suddenly seemed to me a reflection of my own life. I was able to recognise myself in them: with some of them I had a lot in common and with others I didn't, but I was able to recognise a little of myself in those too. It is a question of decisions. A question of hypotheses. And of opportunities – at least, I think it is. And that is also freedom in a way.

The hours pass. I look at my picture. It is an original. I examine it and, when I close my eyes I can see it in my mind's eye. They say that, on average, the normal museum visitor only spends about one-and-a-half minutes in front of a work of art. That's ninety seconds. Sometimes ninety seconds can seem like an eternity, can't it?

In the "crows" episode in Akira Kurosawa's film *Dreams*, a Japanese art student (as Kurosawa's alter ego) is standing in front van Gogh's painting *The Bridge at Langlois near Arles*. In the next shot, the young man is walking around in the very same landscape that he had previously been studying so intensely. There he encounters van Gogh (played by Martin Scorsese) standing at the easel. However, van Gogh soon disappears in the cornfields. The student sets off in search of him and ends up in the world of van Gogh's imagery. Thanks to some remarkable special effects, the viewer sees the young man walking through the painted motifs, disappearing behind houses, crossing the street.

Whilst I am standing in front of my picture, a long-forgotten memory resurfaces in my mind of a scene when I was a child visiting a museum, for the very first time, with my mother. Shush… be very, very quiet, my mother whispered. But while we were standing in front of a painting by Hieronymous Bosch, I suddenly became so afraid that I began to cry. But it's only a painting, said my mother. Really?

Imagine the following situation: it is very late. You are standing at the window again. If someone were to ask you now what your painting was really about, and what it is you find so fascinating about it, you could tell a story, a story that explains a fair amount, but not everything. And you'd really enjoy doing just that. And perhaps you'd then call the night porter and ask him who had painted the picture hanging in your room. And you'd insist on finding it out that very evening, because tomorrow, you would know, tomorrow might be another day. Now, sleep well and dream of it. Of what? Of anything you want. Goodnight.

"o.T.", Jo Schöpfer; Beispiel für eine der Skulpturen
in den Aufzugslobbies der IV. VII. bis Etage

Untitled, Jo Schöpfer; Example of one of the sculptures
in the lift lobbies on the 4th-7th floors.

Appendix

GRAND HYATT BERLIN

Gepäckschein/Luggage Tag

Name/Name

Zimmer Nr./Room No.

Anzahl Gepäckstücke/
Number of Items

013191

The Authors:

Hubertus Adam was born in Hanover in 1965. He studied art history, philosophy and archeology in Heidelberg. From 1997-98, he was on the editorial staff of the *Bauwelt* magazine in Berlin. Since 1998 he has been the editor of *archithese* in Zurich. He also contributes articles (architecture, art and design) as a freelancer for the *Neue Zürcher Zeitung* newspaper and also works as a freelance historian and author. Apart from having architectural reviews published in various daily newspapers and specialist journals, he has also written numerous articles and contributions for catalogues, especially on the subject of 20th century architecture, the art of expressionism, monuments and memorials.

Mechthild Heuser was born in Lünen, Westphalia, in 1964. She studied art history, classical archeology and urban construction at the University of Bonn; obtained her doctorate in art history at the Humboldt University in Berlin with her dissertation: "The Art of the Fugue – From the AEG Turbine Factory to the Illinois Institute of Technology: The Steel Skeleton as an Aesthetic Category" (studies on the industrial architecture of Peter Behrens and its subsequent impact; Mies van der Rohe's late work in America). She received a DAAD (German Academic Exchange Service) research scholarship for the USA and subsequently obtained a Ph.D. scholarship from the Studienstiftung des Deutschen Volkes (Study Foundation of the German People).

She has also worked as a freelance member of the academic staff at the Bonn Art Museum, and at the Art and Exhibition Hall of the Federal Republic of Germany/ Bonn. She was a research assistant at the Museum of Modern Art, New York for the Lilly Reich exhibition staged in 1995. From 1997 on, she began working as a freelance journalist for architecture (articles and photographs) for *Der Architekt*, *Bauwelt*, *Casabella* and *Archithese*. Since 1998, Mechthild Heuser has been a member of the academic staff at the Department of Architecture at the ETH in Zurich, from 1998/9, under Professor Dr. Vittorio Magnago Lampugnani, and has been working under Professor Arthur Rüegg since 1999.

Dorothea Strauss, was born in Braunlage (Germany) in 1960, took art history and theatre, film and television studies in Frankfurt am Main. Since 1996, she has been director of the Kunsthalle St. Gallen and lecturer of art history and art theory at the departments of fine arts and theory of design and art at the Academy of Art and Design, Zurich. Among those she has organised exhibitions with are: Art & Language, Rirkrit Tiravanija, Cosima von Bonin, Noritoshi Hirakawa, Fabrice Hybert, Carsten Höller, Michel Auder, Tamara Grcic, Monika Baer, Nader, Gert Rappenecker, Jonathan Meese, Christoph Büchel, Claudia Di Gallo.

Die Autoren:

Hubertus Adam: geboren 1965 in Hannover; Studium der Kunstgeschichte, Philosophie und Archäologie in Heidelberg. 1997/98 Redakteur der Zeitschrift «Bauwelt» in Berlin, seit 1998 Redakteur der «archithese» in Zürich. Darüber hinaus ständiger freier Mitarbeiter der Neuen Zürcher Zeitung (Architektur, Kunst, Design) sowie Tätigkeit als freier Kunsthistoriker und Autor. Neben Architekturkritiken in diversen Tageszeitungen und Fachzeitschriften zahlreiche wissenschaftliche Aufsätze und Katalogbeiträge, vor allem zu den Themen Architektur des Zwanzigsten Jahrhunderts, Kunst des Expressionismus, Denkmal und Memoria.

Mechthild Heuser: geboren 1964 in Lünen/Westf.; Studium der Kunstgeschichte, Klassischen Archäologie und des Städtebaus an der Universität Bonn; Promotion im Fach Kunstgeschichte an der Humboldt-Universität Berlin zum Thema «Die Kunst der Fuge – Von der AEG Turbinenfabrik zum Illinois Institute of Technology: Das Stahlskelett als ästhetische Kategorie» (=Studie zur Industriearchitektur von Peter Behrens u. deren Nachwirkung im amerikanischen Spätwerk Mies van der Rohes); DAAD-Forschungsstipendium USA; danach Promotionsstipendium der Studienstiftung des Deutschen Volkes. Parallel u. im Anschluß: Freie Tätigkeit als Mitarbeiterin des museumspädagogischen Dienstes des Bonner Kunstmuseums u. der Kunst- und Ausstellungshalle der BRD/ Bonn; Research Assistent am Museum of Modern Art, New York im Rahmen der 1995 präsentierten Lilly-Reich-Ausstellung; Seit 1997 freie Architekturjournalistin (Text u. Fotografie) für «Der Architekt», «Bauwelt», «Casabella», «Archithese». Seit 1998 Wissenschaftliche Assistentin an der Architekturabteilung der ETH-Zürich, 1998/9 am Lehrstuhl von Prof. Dr. Vittorio Magnago Lampugnani, seit 1999 am Lehrstuhl von Prof. Arthur Rüegg.

Dorothea Strauss: geboren 1960 in Braunlage, studierte Kunstgeschichte und Theater-, Film- und Fernsehwissenschaften in Frankfurt am Main. Seit 1996 leitet sie die Kunsthalle St.Gallen und ist Dozentin für Kunstgeschichte und Kunsttheorie in den Studienbe-reichen Bildende Kunst und Theorie der Gestaltung und Kunst an der Hochschule für Gestaltung und Kunst, Zürich, HGKZ. Ausstellungen u.a. mit Art & Language, Rirkrit Tiravanija, Cosima von Bonin, Noritoshi Hirakawa, Fabrice Hybert, Carsten Höller, Michel Auder, Tamara Grcic, Monika Baer, Nader, Gert Rappenecker, Jonathan Meese, Christoph Büchel, Claudia Di Gallo.

Jose Rafael Moneo

JOSE RAFAEL MONEO was born in Tudela, Navarra (Spain) in 1937.

He obtained his architectural degree in 1961 from the Technical School of Architecture in Madrid.

Rafael Moneo is a member of the American Academy of Arts and Sciences, member of the Accademia di San Luca di Roma and member of the Swedish Royal Academy of Fine Arts. He is an Honorary Fellow of the American Institute of Architects and the Royal Institute of British Architects.

Exhibitions

In 1976 Rafael Moneo was invited to the U.S. as Visiting Fellow by the Institute for Architecture and Urban Studies of New York City (1976 / 77) and by the Cooper Union, School of Architecture (NYC 1976 / 77). During the late seventies and early eighties, he was a Visiting Professor at the schools of architecture of Princeton and Harvard universities in the U.S. and later at the architecture department of the Ecole Polytechnique Fédérale in Lausanne, Switzerland. In 1985, Rafael Moneo was named Chairman of the Architecture Department of the Harvard University Graduate School of Design, a position he held until 1990. He remains active as professor at this university and was named Josep Lluís Sert Professor of Architecture in 1991.

Prof. Moneo's pedagogical activities have extended to numerous symposia and lectures. In tandem, Rafael Moneo has developed an extensive body of work as architectural critic and theoretician. His collected writings will in the future be published by CLUVA in Milan, Italy, and by the M.I.T. Press in Cambridge, Massachusetts. The majority of the texts gathered in these volumes were first published in *Oppositions* and *Lotus* magazines, and in *Arquitectura Bis* – an architecture journal co-founded by Rafael Moneo.

Recent exhibitions of the architect's work have taken place at The Art Institute of Chicago, Oct. 1992 ("Building in a New Spain: Contemporary Spanish Architecture"); The Museo Cantonale d'Arte, Lugano, Switzerland, Sept.1992 ("Art Museums and Architecture"); Ministerio de Obras Públicas y Transportes, Madrid, Oct.1992 ("Ten Years of Spanish Architecture 1980–1990"); at the Círculo de Bellas Artes, Madrid, May 1994 ("Museums and Architecture"); A monographic exhibition of the architect's work from the start of his career has taken place in the spring of 1993 at the Akademie der Bildenden Künste of Vienna ("Rafael Moneo, Building in the City"); in the summer of 1993 at the Architekturmuseum in Basel ("Rafael Moneo, Buildings and Projects 1976–1992"); in the autumn of 1993 in the Arkitekturmuseet in Stockholm ("Rafael Moneo, Buildings and Projects 1973–1993") and in the autumn of 1994 in the Museum of Finnish Architecture in Helsinki.

JOSE RAFAEL MONEO wurde 1937 in Tudela, Navarra (Spanien) geboren.

Seine architektonische Ausbildung erhielt er an der Technischen Universiät in Madrid.

Rafael Moneo ist Mitglied der «American Academy of Arts and Sciences», der «Accademia di San Luca» in Rom und der «Königlichen Akademie der Künste» von Schweden. Er ist Ehrenmitglied des «American Institute of Architects» und des «Royal Institute of Architects».

Ausstellungen

1976 wurde Rafael Moneo als Gastprofessor vom «Institute for Architecture and Urban Studies» (NYC 1976 / 77) und der «Cooper Union» eingeladen. Während der späten siebziger, Anfang der achtziger Jahre war er Gastprofessor an den Architektur-fakultäten in Princeton und Harvard, nachfolgend an der «École Polytechnique» in Lausanne (Schweiz). 1985 wurde Rafael Moneo zum Vorsteher der Architekturfakultät in Harvard; eine Position die er bis 1990 innehatte. Durch die ihm zugesprochene Lluis Sert Professur ist er bis heute dieser Universität aktiv verbunden.

Die ungezählten Lehrveranstaltungen von Prof. Moneo umfassen Symposien und Vorträge. In diesem Zusammenhang hat Rafael Moneo auch ein umfangreiches Œuvre als Kritiker und Theoretiker vorgelegt. Eine Sammlung seiner Texte wird gegenwärtig von «CLUVA» (Mailand) und der «MIT-Press» in Cambridge (Massachusetts, USA) vorbereitet. Ein Großteil dieser Texte erschien zuerst in «Oppositions» und «Lotus», sowie «Arquitectura Bis», einer von Rafael Moneo mitbegründeten Zeitschrift.

Ausstellungen der jüngeren Vergangenheit waren zu sehen im «Art Institute of Chicago»; im Oktober 1992 («Building in a New Spain: Contemporary Spanish Architecture»); dem «Museo Cantonale d'Arte» in Lugano, Schweiz, im September 1992 («;Art Museums and Architecture»); dem «Ministerio de Obras Publicas y Transportes, Madrid», im Oktober 1992 («10 Years of Spanish Architecture 1980–1990») und dem «Circulo de Bellas Artes», Madrid im Mai 1994 («Museums and Architecture»). Eine monographische Werkübersicht war im Frühjahr 1993 an der «Akademie der Bildenden Künste» in Wien zu sehen («Rafael Moneo, Bauen in der Stadt»); im Sommer im «Architekturmuseum Basel» («Rafael Moneo, Bauten und Projekte 1976–1992»), im Herbst im «Arkitekturmuseet» in Stockholm («Rafael Moneo, Buildings and Projects 1973–1993»;) und im darauffolgenden Frühjahr im «Museum of Finnish Architecture» in Helsinki.

Hannes Wettstein

*1958 Ascona/Switzerland	*1958 Ascona/Schweiz
Product Design, Corporate Design, Interior Design, Architecture	Formgebung, Corporate Design, Raumgestaltung, Architektur

Büro für Gestaltung, Zurich/CH, design studio: free-lance work	1982-1988	Büro für Gestaltung, Zürich/CH: selbständige Tätigkeit
Foundation of the "Diesseits" edition (small series and unique pieces)	1989	Gründung der Edition «Diesseits» (Kleinserien und Unikate)
Eclat, Design Agency, Erlenbach/CH: co-partner and head of the 3D sector	1989-1991	Eclat, Designagentur, Erlenbach/CH: Mitinhaber und Leitung des 3D-Bereichs
Guest lecturer at colleges and schools: Gerrit Rietveld Academie Amsterdam/NL, Technical College Hannover/Germany, F.F.I. Basel/CH, Piccola scuola di design Milano/I, Centro Europeo di Design Milano/I	1990-1995 1991-1996	Gastdozent an Akademien und Schulen: Gerrit Rietveld Academie Amsterdam/NL Fachhochschule Hannover/D, F.F.I.Basel/CH, Piccola Scuola di Design Milano/I, Centro Europeo di Design Milano/I
Lecturer at the Swiss Federal Institute of Technologie (ETH) Zurich/CH	1992	Dozent an der ETH Zürich/CH
Foundation of [zed]. design network	1992	Gründung von [zed]. design network
Member of the jury for the Applied Art Scholarship of the Canton of Lucerne/CH	1994	Jurymitglied des Stipendiums für angewandte Kunst des Kantons Luzern/CH
9D Design Zurich/CH: co-founder and partner	since 1993	9D Design Zürich/CH: Mitbegründer und Partner
Professor at the Academy of Design in Karlsruhe/Germany	since 1994	Professor an der Hochschule für Gestaltung Karlsruhe/D

Exhibitions and awards		**Ausstellungen und Auszeichnungen**
Exhibition "Neue Designtendenzen" (New Design Trends), Milano/I	1983	Ausstellung «Neue Designtendenzen», Mailand/I
Workshop-Exhibition "Unverrichtete Dinge" (Undone Things), Margine Gallery, Zurich/CH	1985	Werkausstellung «Unverrichtete Dinge» in der Galerie Margine, Zürich/CH
Exhibition "Spider Multiples" – Playing with Mannerism and Geometry, Zurich/CH	1989	Ausstellung «Spider Multiples» – ein Spiel mit Manierismen und Geometrien, Zürich/CH
Workshop-Exhibitions: Krämer, Winterthur/CH; Binnen Gallery, Amsterdam/NL	1990	Werkausstellungen: Krämer, Winterthur/CH; Galerie Binnen, Amsterdam/NL
VSI-Prize for furniture design, Switzerland, participation in the exhibition "Mehrwerte – Schweizer Design der 80er Jahre" (Added Values – 80s Design in Switzerland) at the Museum für Gestaltung, Zurich/CH	1990 1991	VSI-Preis für Möbelgestaltung, Schweiz Teilnahme an der Ausstellung «Mehrwerte – Schweizer Design der 80er Jahre» im Museum für Gestaltung, Zürich/CH
Exhibition Project "Selbstbedienung" (Self-Service) with "CeHa" and "Diesseits", within the context of the "Designhorizonte" exhibition, Frankfurt/D	1991	Ausstellungsprojekt «Selbstbedienung» mit «CeHa» und «Diesseits» im Rahmen der «Designhorizonte», Frankfurt/D
Contest "Raumvisionen" (Space Visions), AIT-Prize, Germany	1992	Wettbewerb «Raumvisionen», AIT-Preis, Deutschland
First prize in the contest "Öffentliche Uhren in der Stadt Frankfurt" (Public clocks in the city of Frankfurt), Germany Award "Compasso d'Oro ADI", Milano/I, for "Caprichair"	1994	1.Preis im Wettbewerb «Öffentliche Uhren in der Stadt Frankfurt», D Auszeichnung «Compasso d'Oro ADI», Mailand/I, für «Caprichair»
Awards for "V-Matic" chronometer: "Höchste Designqualität", Design-Zentrum Nordrhein Westfalen/D; "Industrie Forum Design award", Hannover/D; "Design Plus", Frankfurt/D; "Good Design", Chicago/USA.	1995	Auszeichnungen für Chronometer «V-Matic»: «Höchste Designqualität», Design-Zentrum Nordrhein Westfalen/D; «Industrie Forum Design Award», Hannover/D; «Design Plus», Frankfurt/D; «Good Design», Chicago/USA.
Award "Höchste Designqualität", Design-Zentrum Nordrhein Westfalen/D, for lighting system "Cyos"	1996	Auszeichnung für «Höchste Designqualität», Design-Zentrum Nordrhein Westfalen/D, für Beleuchtungssystem «Cyos»
International Design Prize "Langlebigkeit" Baden-Württemberg/D, for V-Matic	1996/97	Internationaler Designpreis «Langlebigkeit» des Landes Baden-Württemberg/D für V-Matic

Ort: **Lobby** o.T., Berlin 1988; Casein auf Leinwand 80 x 400 cm (mit 2 Sofittenlampen
betec , 88 cm, die parallel mittelachsig über dem Bild angebracht sind)

Location: **Lobby** *Untitled*, Berlin 1988, casein on canvas, 80 x 400 cm (with 2 tubular lamps,
88 cm, hung parallel to one another above the middle of the picture.

John Armleder

JOHN ARMLEDER, wurde 1948 in Genf geboren; lebt und arbeitet in Genf.

Born 1948 in Geneva; lives and works in Geneva.

Einzelausstellungen seit / Solo Shows since 1991

1999   "At any Speed", Holderbank, Aarau (K)

1998/1999   "At any Speed", Kunsthalle Baden-Baden (K)
The Box,Torino
"Dont't do it!", Galerie Anselm Dreher, Berlin
ACE Gallery, Los Angeles/New York
"Mondo Tiki II", Galerie Tanit, München
"Œuvres 1967/1997", Galerie Brownstone, Corréard & Cie, Paris

1998   "Works on Paper 1967–1998", Galerie Susanna Kulli, St. Gallen
"Rewind, Fast Forward, Any Speed", Galerie Mehdi Chouakri, Berlin
"Wall Paintings 1967–1998" Casino, Luxembourg
Galerie Erna Mecey, Luxembourg
Artspace, Auckland

1997   "Peintures murales 1967–1997", La Box, Bourges
"Le Parvis", Ibos-Pau
"Perspex Sculptures", Galerie Gilbert Brownstone, Paris

1996   Galerie Susanna Kulli, St. Gallen
Galerie Jean-Franois Dumont, Bordeaux
Galerie Art & Public, Genève
Galerie Tanit, München
Galerie Sollertis, Toulouse
Galeria Gracinda, Lisboa
Galerie Art & Public, Genève
Galerie Susanna Kulli, St. Gallen
ECAL, Lausanne
"Territorio Italiano", Piacenza
Galerie 360, Tokyo
Galerie Klaus Nordenhake, Stockholm

1995   UBS, Schloss Wolfsberg, Ermatingen
"L'œuvre multiplié", Cabinet des Estampes du Musée d'art et d'histoire, Genève
Centre d'art contemporain, Abbaye Saint-André, Meymac
Centre d'art contemporain, La Maison, Douai
Galerie Klaus Nordenhake, Stockholm
Galerie MDJ, art contemporain, Neuchâtel
Galerie Sfeir-Semmler, Kiel
Galerie Massimo de Carlo, Milano
Galerie Air de Paris, Jean-Franois Dumont, Paris

1994   Galerie Art & Public, Genève
"Les Assiettes", Daniel Baumann & CLPV, Thenex
Centre d'Art Contemporain, Le Capitou, Fréjus
Galerie Sollertis, Toulouse
CB Art Gallery, Sydney

1993   "Travaux sur Papier 1967–1992", Galerie Marika
Malacorda, Genève
Galerie Gilbert Brownstone, Paris
Wiener Secession, Wien
Villa Arson, CNAC, Nice
Galerie Daniel Newburg, New York
Galerie Catherine Issert, Saint-Paul-de-Vence
Les Entrepts Laydet, Paris
Centre Genevois de Gravure Contemporaine, Genève

1992   Galerie Sollertis, Toulouse
Centre Culturel de Dax, Dax
"Pour Paintings 1989–1992", Centraal Museum, Utrecht
"Works on Paper 1966–1992", Centraal Museum, Utrecht
Galleria Massimo de Carlo, Milano
John Gibson Gallery, New York

1991   Galerie Paolo Vitolo Contemporanea, Roma
Galerie Porte-Avion, Marseille
Galerie Marika Malacorda, Genève
John Gibson Gallery, New York
Daniel Newburg Gallery, New York
Castello di Rivara, Torino
Galerie Trésor d'Art, Gstaad
Galerie van Gelder, Amsterdam

(K) = Katalog / Catalog

Location: **Lobby / corridors** *Wooden Buoy* (1992), various types of wood   *Spindel I* (1995); various types of wood   Ort: **Lobby / Flure** Holzboje (1992); verschiedene Holzarten   Spindel I (1995); verschiedene Holzarten
Lead Buoy (1991); wood in lead casing   *Spindel II* (1995); various types of wood   Bleiboje (1991); Holz mit Blei ummantelt   Spindel II (1995); verschiedene
Iron Buoy (1997); cast iron   Eisenboje (1997); Gusseisen   Holzarten

Ingrid Hartlieb

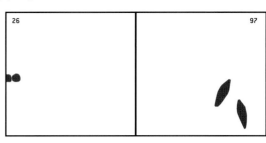

INGRID HARTLIEB wurde 1944 in Reichenberg (CR) geboren; 1980 Preis der Darmstädter Sezession; 1982 Arbeitsstipendium des Landes Baden-Württemberg in Olevano-Romano (I); 1985–1989 Lehrauftrag an der Fachhochschule für Gestaltung, Pforzheim; 1986 Lovis-Corinth-Förderpreis der Künstlergilde Esslingen; 1988 Arbeitsaufenthalt in Chicago mit Unterstützung der Kunststiftung Baden-Württemberg; 1989–1990 Studienaufenthalt Cité Internationale des Arts, Paris; 1995 Arbeits-aufenthalt im Socrates Sculpture Park, Long Island City (New York); 1998 Workshop am Technikon Natal, Durban (Südafrika); lebt und arbeitet in Stuttgart.

Born 1944 in Reichenberg (CR); lives and works in Stuttgart.

Einzelausstellungen seit / Solo Shows since 1985

1998   Galerie Schieper, Hagen
Sammlung G E, Süderlügum
Galerie Angelika Hathan, Stuttgart
Kilianskirche, Heilbronn
Technikon Natal Art Gallery, Durban

1997   Bianca Lanza, Miami

1996   Kulturforum, Schorndorf
Schloss Monrepos '96, Ludwigsburg (K)

1995   Bianca Lanza Gallery, Miami
Laupmeier Sculpture Park and Museum, St.Louis
Zapata, Kunst und Kultur, Stuttgart

1994   Kunstverein Eislingen
Oskar Fiedl Gallery, Chicago
University of Wisconsin Art Museum, Milwaukee
Galerie Schloss Haigerloch
Marktgalerie, Horb

1993   Gerhard Marcks Haus, Bremen (K)

1992   Galerie am Friedrichsplatz, Mannheim
Galerie Hartl und Klier, Tübingen

1991   Institut Français, Stuttgart
THE Gallery, New York
Oskar Friedl Gallery, Chicago
Galerie Radetzky und Gierig, München

1990   Siemens Zweigniederlassung, Stuttgart (K)
Galerie Municipale Eduard Manet, Gennevilliers / Paris (K)
Wilhelmshöhe e.V., Ettlingen (mit P. Koch)
Galerie Schloß Haigerloch

1989   Kunstverein Unna
Trabica-McAfee-Gallery, New York
Galerie Tendenz, Sindelfingen
Kunststation St.Peter, Köln
Städtische Galerie, Tuttlingen
Oskar Friedl Gallery, Chicago

1988   Akademie der Diözese Rottenburg, Stuttgart

1987   Kunstverein Ludwigshafen (K)

1986   Galerie Timm Gierig, Frankfurt a. M.
Galerie Hartl und Klier, Tübingen
Kreissparkasse, Göppingen

1985   Mannheimer Kunstverein (Luisenpark), Mannheim
Städtische Galerie Wendlingen a.N. (mit H. Koch)
Galerie Lüpfert, Hannover-Isernhagen

Ort: **Library** o.T., 1997 / 1998; fünfteilige Arbeit (Acryllack, auf MDF verleimt), unterschiedliche Maße

Location: **Library** *Untitled*, 1997 / 1998; five-part work (acrylic, glued to MDF); of varying dimensions.

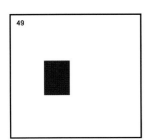

Kurt Hofmann

KURT HOFMANN wurde 1954 in Stuttgart geboren; 1977–1983 Studium an der Kunstakademie Stuttgart; 1987 Reinhold Kurth-Kunstpreis der Frankfurter Sparkasse; lebt und arbeitet in Frankfurt a. M.

Born 1954 in Stuttgart; lives and works in Frankfurt a. M.

Einzelausstellungen / Solo Shows

1994	Ausstellungshalle Zoo in Zusammenarbeit mit dem MMK, Frankfurt a. M.

1989   Galerie Luis Campaña, Frankfurt a. M.

1992   Galerie Luis Campaña, Frankfurt a. M.

1987   Galerie Anselm Dreher, Berlin
Förderkoje "ART COLOGNE", Galerie Anselm Dreher, Berlin

1991   Galerie Luis Campaña, Frankfurt a. M.

Ort: **Lobby** «ready mix (a)1»; 1998, Aluminium / Lack (400 x 300 x 30 cm; 250 kg)

Location: **Lobby** *Ready mix* (a)1; 1998, aluminium / paint (400 x 300 x 30cm, 250kg).

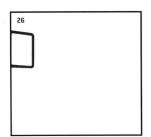

Gerold Miller

GEROLD MILLER wurde 1961 in Altshausen / Ravensburg geboren; 1984–1989 Studium der Bildhauerei an der Staatlichen Akademie der Bildenden Künste Stuttgart bei Jürgen Brodwolf; 1986 Akademiepreis; 1989–1992 Atelierstipendium des Landes Baden-Württemberg; 1990 Stipendium der Kunststiftung Baden-Württemberg; Stipendium des DAAD für Chicago / USA; 1991–1995 Gruppe L; 1991 Arbeitsaufenthalt in New York und Chicago; 1994 / 1995 Stipendium Cité Internationale des Arts Paris; 1998 Arbeitsaufenthalt im Miedzynarodowe Centrum Sztuki, Poznan; lebt und arbeitet in Berlin.

Born 1961 in Altshausen/Ravensburg; lives and works in Berlin.

Einzelausstellungen / Solo Shows

1996   Galerie Albrecht, München; Kunsthalle Winterthur (K);
"Some paintings and a jacket", CBD Gallery, Sydney
Galerie Kästring / Maier, München (mit Jean-Luc Manz)

1999   ON Galeria, Poznan; Galerie Albrecht; München; Artspace Sydney;
PS Amsterdam

1995/1996   Bahnwärterhaus, Galerie der Stadt Esslingen (K)

1995   "Retour de Paris", Institut Français, Stuttgart

1998   Kunstverein Bochum, "2 Anlagen, 4 Stühle und 1 Bier"; Büro 2plus, Nürnberg;
"Someone else's studio", Studio Gail Hastings, Brisbane;
Galerie Anselm Dreher, Berlin

1994   Kunstraum G7, Mannheim

1993   Galerie im Kornhaus der Stadt Kirchheim / Teck,
(mit Simone Westerwinter)

1997   "Anlagen", Städtische Galerie Altes Theater, Ravensburg (K); "Wall as Medium", Institute of Modern Art, Brisbane; Studio im Museum am Ostwall, Dortmund (K); David Pestorius Gallery, Brisbane; "Project", Sarah Cottier Gallery, Brisbane; Galerie Albrecht, München (mit Simone Westerwinter); "Leere Versprechungen, hast Du gesagt", Stadtgalerie im Sophienhof, Kiel (K); Städtische Galerie, Villingen-Schwenningen (K)

1992   Galerie der Kunststiftung Baden-Württemberg, Stuttgart
Galerie im Kornhaus der Stadt Kirchheim / Teck

1989   Torschlossgalerie Tettnang

1997   Galerie der Stadt Fellbach

1996/1997   "Anlagen und Gummitwist", Galerie Achim Kubinski, Stuttgart

(K) = Katalog / Catalog

Location: **Boardroom** *Around M.D.*, four works, oil crayon on fabric, paint behind glass (60 x 60cm each).

Ort: **Boardroom** "Around M.D.", 4 Arbeiten, Ölkreiden auf Stoff, Lack hinter Glas (je 60 x 60 cm)

Julio Rondo

JULIO RONDO wurde 1952 in Sotrondio (Spanien) geboren; lebt und arbeitet in Stuttgart.

Born 1952 in Sotrondio (Spain); lives and works in Stuttgart.

Einzelausstellungen (Auswahl) seit / Solo Shows (selection) since 1987

1999   Gasser + Grunert Gallery, New York (K); Galerie Andreas Binder, München (K)

1998   Galerie Reinhard Hauff, Stuttgart (K)

1997   Galerie Andreas Binder, München

1996   Galerie Tanja Grunert, Köln; Galerie Reinhard Hauff, Stuttgart

1995   Galerie Klaus Peter Göbel, Stuttgart (K)

(K) = Katalog / Catalog

1993   Galerie Tanja Grunert, Köln

1991   Galerie Ralph Wernicke, Stuttgart (K); Galerie Wilma Tolksdorf, Hamburg

1990   Galerie Tanja Grunert, Köln; Galerie Marc Jancou, Zürich

1989   Galerie Wilma Tolksdorf, Hamburg

1988   Galerie Tanja Grunert, Köln; Galerie Ralph Wernicke Stuttgart (K)

1987   Kunstraum Stuttgart

Location: **Corridors** Four sculptures, untitled, 1994, 1997, 2 x 1998, bronze cast, unica

Ort: **Flure** 4 Skulpturen, o.T., 1994, 1997, 2x 1998; Bronzeguß; Unikate Maße: 34 x 48,5 x 37cm; 33 x 37 x 33cm; 46 x 19 x 11,5cm; 30 x 39 x 31cm

Jo Schöpfer

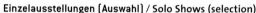

JO SCHÖPFER wurde 1951 in Coburg geboren; 1974–80 Studium an der Staatlichen Akademie der Bildenden Künste in Stuttgart; 1985 Stipendium der Kunststiftung Baden-Württemberg; 1987–1988 Stipendium der Deutschen Akademie Villa Massimo in Rom, 1989 Arbeitsstipendium des Kunstfonds e.V., Bonn; lebt und arbeitet in Berlin.

Born 1951 in Coburg; lives and works in Berlin.

Einzelausstellungen (Auswahl) / Solo Shows (selection)

1999   Niederrheinischer Kunstverein, Kalkar; Galerie Michael Zink, Regensburg

1998   Freundeskreis Wilhelmshöhe, Ettlingen

1997   Galerie Edith Wahlandt, Stuttgart; Galerie der Stadt Sindelfingen (K)

1996   Galerie Michael Zink, Regensburg; Kunstverein Heilbronn (K); Museum Folkwang, Essen (K); Galerie Klaus Fischer, Berlin

1995   Elke Dröscher, Kunstraum Fleetinsel, Hamburg; Städtische Galerie Regensburg (K); Galerie Michael Zink, Regensburg; Städtische Galerie, Altes Theater, Ravensburg (K)

1993   Galerie Tilly Hadtrek, Stuttgart; Galerie Klaus Fischer, Berlin; Zeche Zollverein, Essen

1992   Galerie am Fischmarkt, Erfurt (K); Museo Comunale, Rimini (K)

1991   Galerie Heimeshoff – Jochen Krüper, Essen; Städtische Galerie, Göppingen (K)

1989   Galleria Nuova Pesa, Roma (K)

1988   Kunstforum; Städtische Galerie im Lenbachhaus, München (K); PAC (Padiglione d'Arte Contemporanea) Milano (K); Galleria Nicola Verlato, Bologna

1987   Galerie Beatrix Wilhelm, Stuttgart (K)

1986   Hans Thoma-Gesellschaft, Reutlingen (K); Galerie Heimeshoff – Jochen Krüper, Essen (K)

1985   Galerie Achim Kubinski, Stuttgart (K)

1983   Galerie Tanja Grunert, Stuttgart

(K) = Katalog / Catalog

Ort: **Lobby (1 OG)** o.T., Öl auf Leinwand; 170 x 290 cm | Location: **Lobby** *Untitled*, oil on canvas, 170 x 290 cm.

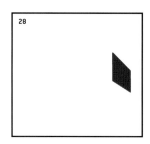

Dirk Skreber

DIRK SKREBER wurde 1961 in Lübeck geboren; 1982–1988 Studium an der Kunstakademie Düsseldorf (bei Alfonso Hüppi); 1994 /1995 Gastprofessur an der Kunstakademie Karlsruhe; 1996 Gastseminar an der Kunstakademie Malmö; lebt und arbeitet in Düsseldorf.

Born 1961 in Lübeck; lives and works in Düsseldorf.

Einzelausstellungen (Auswahl) / Solo Shows (selection)

1994	Bloom Gallery, Amsterdam; Kunsthalle Rostock (K)
1992	Kunstraum München(K); Bloom Gallery, Amsterdam
1991	Galerie Schmela, Düsseldorf
1989	Galerie Schmela, Düsseldorf
1988	Galerie Schmela, Düsseldorf

1999	Luis Campaña, Köln; Blum & Poe, Los Angeles
1998	Portfolio, Wien
1997	Galerie Bochynek, Düsseldorf; Leopold-Hoesch-Museum, Düren (K); Luis Campaña, Köln
1996	Galerie Steir-Semmler, Kiel

Ort: **Lobby (1 OG)** Wandzeichnung | Location: **Lobby** Wall drawing

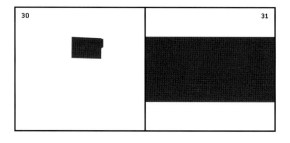

Otto Zitko

OTTO ZITKO wurde 1959 in Linz geboren; 1977–1982 Studium an der Hochschule für angewandte Kunst, Wien; 1996 Msgr. Otto Mauer Preis; lebt und arbeitet in Wien.

Born 1959 in Linz; lives and works in Vienna.

Einzelausstellungen (Auswahl) seit / Solo Shows (selection) since 1983

1992	Wiener Secession, Wien (K); Peter Pakesch Galerie, Wien; Galerie Rodolphe Janssen, Brüssel
1991	Jänner Galerie, Wien (K)
1990	Galerie Grässlin-Erhardt, Frankfurt a. M.; Galerie Eugen Lendl, Graz Galerie Stadtpark, Krems (K); Stichting de Appel, Amsterdam (mit Franz West) (K)
1989	Galerie Peter Pakesch, Wien
1987	Galerie Peter Pakesch, Wien (K)
1986	Galerie Borgmann-Capitain, Köln; "Für uns menschliche Tiere", ORF, Graz
1985	Galerie Albert Baronian, Knogge; Galerie Jean Bernier (mit Herbert Brandl), Athens; Galerie Peter Pakesch, Wien

1999	Galerie E & K Thoman, Innsbruck; Rupertinum, Salzburg
1998	Galerie F. Figl, Linz
1997	Galerie E & K Thoman, Innsbruck (K)
1996	Galerie Christine König, Wien
1995	Galerie am Stein, Schärding; Galerie Rodolphe Janssen, Brüssel; Galerie Potocka, Krakau
1994	Kunsthalle Bern (K); Künstlerhaus, Klagenfurt (K); Galerie der Stadt Wels (K); Galerie A4, Wels; Kunstverein Hamburg (K); Fassadenprojekt Nr. 4, Culturcentrum Wolkenstein; Trabant, Wien (Raumzeichnung)
1993	Galerie F. Figl, Linz; Galerie Na bidylku, Brünn (K)

(K) = Katalog / Catalog

Projektdaten
Project Data

Offizelle Projektbezeichnung **Official name of the project:**	Grand Hyatt Hotel **Grand Hyatt Hotel**
Ort **Location:**	Marlene-Dietrich-Platz 2; Berlin Deutschland / Germany
Auftraggeber **Client:**	debis Immobilienmanagement GmbH
Architekt **Architect:**	José Rafael Moneo, Madrid
Partner-Architekten **Associate Architects:** **Project Manager:**	Chwalisz + Sieg, Mory, Osterwalder, Vielmo AP Plan GmbH, Berlin Volker Sieg
Raumgestaltung **Interior Design:**	Hannes Wettstein, Zürich **(Ballroom, Ballroom-Bar, Conference-Rooms,** **Restaurants, Health-Club, Room-Furniture,** **Art-Concept)** Dani Freixes, Barcelona (Bistro »Dietrich's«)
Projektgröße **Project Area:**	30,000 m²; inkl/incl. 300 Standardzimmer / **Standard-Rooms** 41 Suiten / **Suites (incl. 12 Singlebed and** 18 Mini-Suiten / **Suites)** Tizian-Restaurant für / **for 80** Personen / **Persons** Vox-Restaurant für / **for 186** Personen / **Persons** 2 Ballsäle für / **Ballrooms for 600** Personen / **Persons** **Boardroom für / Library for 18 Personen /** **Persons** 5 Konferenzräume für / **Conference-Rooms for 245** Personen / **Persons**
Budget	198.5 Mio DM
Zeitraum **Dates:**	1993 (Planungsauftrag im Frühjahr / **Commission in Spring)** 1995 (Grundsteinlegung / **Ground Breaking)** 1998 (Eröffnung / **Inauguration:** Oktober / **October)**

Mitarbeiter / **Collaborators**

Projektleitung Architektur **Project-Architects:**	Filip de Wachter Román Cisneros
Mitarbeiter **Team:**	Juan Beldarrain, Jean-Daniel Boyé, Juan Helvia, Max Holst, Jan Kleihues, Julio Salcedo,
Projektleitung Raumgestaltung **Project-Designers:**	Michael Brönnimann, Ralf Gubler (Suiten)
Mitarbeiter Raumgestaltung **Team:**	Davide Cilesa, Gaby Faeh, Ralf Gubler, Daniel Kübler, Klaus Leuschel, Claudia Meythaler (Graphik)
Projektleitung Kunstkonzept **Art-Project:**	Klaus Leuschel
Beratung (Malerei / Suiten) **Art-Consulting (Paintings / Suites):**	Sophie M. Ott, Zürich
Mitarbeiter **Team:** (verantwortlich vor Ort; **responsible on site)**	Annette Thomas Frank Hautau, Maike von Holdt, Christiane Jungblut, Arndt Kästner, Knut Kruppa, Claudia Meythaler, Dietrich Oberstädt, Petra Ziech

Von Projektbeginn bis zum «Grand Opening» im März 1999 standen den hier namentlich genannten Personen punktuell, speziell, kurz- und längerfristig zahlreiche andere mit Rat und Tat zur Seite, die nicht vergessen sein sollen. Ihnen gilt der Dank der Verantwortlichen ebenso wie allen anderen Wasserträgern: von Essens- über Kurierdienste bis hin zu jenen Erfindern, denen wir erst das Fax-Gerät und das zweite Leben der Maus verdanken, ohne welche die Abwicklung derartiger Projekte heute gar nicht möglich wäre.

From the beginning of the project to the *grand opening* in March 1999, those named here were assisted by countless others, who were there to serve them, in word and deed, at all times and all places, and who should not be forgotten. Those responsible wish to thank them as well as the other dogsbodies: from caterers to messengers to all those inventors who repaired our faxes, breathed a second life into our computer mice, etc., and without whom projects of this nature could never be completed.

Photograph:	**Herbert Bayer**	**Herbert Bayer**	**Herbert Bayer** Fotomontage	**Herbert Bayer**	**Herbert Bayer**
Titel:	"Beine"	"Metamorphosis"	"Profil en face"	"Einsamer Großstädter"	"Stilleben/still life"
Datum:	um 1928	1936	1929	1932	1936
Copyright:	VG Bild Kunst Bonn	VG Bild Kunst Bonn	VG Bild Kunst Bonn	VG Bild Kunst Bonn	VG Bild Kunst Bonn
Bibliographie:	s. Nishen Nr. 78	s. Nishen Nr. 90	s. Nishen Nr. 83	s. Nishen Nr. 87	s. Nishen Nr. 91

 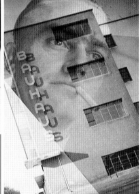 

Photography:	**Florence Henri**	**Kurt Kranz** Doppelbelichtung	**Hannes Meyer**
Title:	"Obst"	"Portrait und Bauhaus"	"Construction 1926/4"
Date:	1929	1930	1926
Copyright:	Galleria Martini @ Ronchetti, Genua, Italien	Ingrid Kranz, Wedel	Claudia Meyer, Zürich
Bibliography:	s. Nishen Nr. 68	s. Nishen Nr. 263	s. Nishen Nr. 410

IV: Appendix: Photographie am Bauhaus

Marianne Brandt

"Spiegelungen"
1928/29
Bauhaus-Archiv GmbH Berlin

Marianne Brandt
Fotocollage
"me"
1927–28
Bauhaus-Archiv GmbH Berlin
s. Nishen Nr. 181

Werner David Feist

"Schirmgestell"
um 1929–30
Ursula Feist, Cote St. Luc, Kanada
s. Nishen Nr. 237

Florence Henri

"Komposition II"
1928
Galleria Martini @ Ronchetti, Genua, Italien
s. Nishen Nr. 63

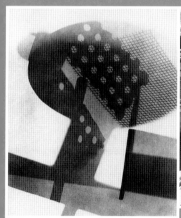

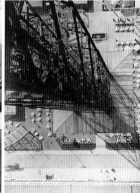

László Moholy-Nagy
Fotogramm
ohne Titel
um 1925-1927
VG Bild Kunst Bonn
s. Nishen Nr. 2

László Moholy-Nagy

"Gangplank from above"
1930
VG Bild Kunst Bonn
s. Nishen Nr. 15

László Moholy-Nagy

"Funkturm Berlin"
1925 (s. Titel)
VG Bild Kunst Bonn
s. Nishen Nr. 6

Lucia Moholy
"Bauhaus Neubau Detailansicht:
Balkon Prellerhaus"
1926
Bauhaus-Archiv Berlin
s. Nishen Nr. 304

Lucia Moholy
"Bauhaus Neubau Dessau,
Werkstättenbau-Spiegelglaskonstruktion"
1926
Bauhaus-Archiv Berlin
s. Nishen Nr. 302

Photograph: **Walter Peterhans**

Titel: "Sektschale", negativ
Datum: um 1928–32
Copyright: Brigitte Peterhans, Chicago
Bibliographie: s. Nishen Nr. 116

Walter Peterhans

"Stilleben mit Gaze und Blüten"
1928–32
Brigitte Peterhans, Chicago
s. Nishen Nr. 114

Gertrud Arndt

ohne Titel
um 1929
Alexa Bormann-Arndt, Darmstadt
s. Nishen S. 98

Gertrud Arndt

"Gläser"
um 1929
Alexa Bormann-Arndt, Darms
s. Nishen S.99

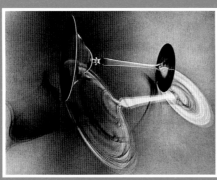   

Photography: **anonym
(Klasse Peterhans)**
Title: "thermosflasche"
Date: um 1929
Copyright: Bauhaus-Archiv Berlin
Bibliography: s. Nishen S.98

**anonym
(Klasse Peterhans)**
ohne Titel
um 1929
Bauhaus-Archiv Berlin
s. Nishen S.99

**anonym
(Klasse Peterhans)**
"baumrinde"
um 1929
Bauhaus-Archiv Berlin
s. Nishen S.99

**anonym
(Klasse Peterhans)**
ohne Titel
um 1929
Bauhaus-Archiv Berlin
s. Nishen S.99

Hinnerk Scheper

ohne Titel
um 1929
Dr. Dirk Scheper, Berlin
s. Nishen S.99

Naphtaly Rubinstein (Avnon)

ohne Titel
um 1929

s. Nishen S.98

**anonym
(Klasse Peterhans)**
ohne Titel
um 1929
Bauhaus-Archiv Berlin
s. Nishen S.98

**anonym
(Klasse Peterhans)**
"landweg"
um 1929
Bauhaus-Archiv Berlin
s. Nishen S.98

**anonym
(Klasse Peterhans)**
ohne Titel
um 1929
Bauhaus-Archiv Berlin
s. Nishen S.98

**Referenzwerk / Reference Book
"Fotografie am Bauhaus"**
Überblick über eine Periode der Fotografie
im 20. Jahrhundert.

Katalog und Ausstellung des
Bauhaus-Archivs Berlin.

Peter Hahn (verantwortl. Herausgeber)
Jeannine Fiedler (Konzeption/Redaktion)
Sabine Hartmann (Mitarbeit) u.a.m.

Verlag Dirk Nishen, Berlin 1990

Herbert Schürmann

"Steine"
1931-33
Grete Schürmann, Velbert

anonym

Balkone des Atelierhauses
1929–30

s. Nishen Nr. 222

Marianne Brandt

Selbstportrait
1928-29
Bauhaus-Archiv GmbH Berlin

Georg Muche

Fotokomposition
1921
Bauhaus-Archiv Berlin
s. Nishen Nr. 231

Ein besonderer Dank geht an Ralf Gubler, Andreas Löhlein und Sophie Ott, ohne deren unermüdlichen Einsatz «die spitzen Winkel in den Balkongittern» nicht wiedergegeben werden könnten.

Our special thanks go to Ralf Gubler, Andreas Löhlein and Sophie Ott, without whose tireless efforts "the acute angles in the balcony railings" could never have been reproduced.

Stand der Biographien: Ende 1999
* = Biographische Angaben; **fett** = Abbildung

Biographies as of end of 1999
* = biographical information, **bold** = illustration